David Livingstone

MAN OF PRAYER AND ACTION

C. Silvester Horne, M.P.

*To David Livingstone, to become a Christian
was to become in spirit and desire, a missionary.*

CHRISTIAN LIBERTY PRESS, ARLINGTON HEIGHTS, ILLINOIS

Copyright © 1999 by Christian Liberty Press

Printed by
Christian Liberty Press
502 West Euclid Avenue
Arlington Heights, Illinois 60004
www.homeschools.org

Revised by Michael J. McHugh
Edited by Edward J. Shewan
Copyediting by Kathleen A. Bristley
Design by Robert Fine
Photos—cover, pages 49-50: Robert Fine

Printed in the United States of America

Preface

It was the great Christian missionary and explorer, David Livingstone, who once said, "I'll go anywhere with God, as long as it is forward." These inspiring words summarize well the whole focus of this pioneer missionary to the African people. Livingstone was gifted with a forward-looking eye that was confident in the power of the Gospel of Christ to change men and nations. He acted upon his faith in full knowledge that the church of Christ would some day batter down the gates of hell.

It is sad to witness the lack of confidence characteristic of many Christian missionaries at the beginning of the twenty-first century. So many who are called to the mission field today expect a meager harvest of souls. They lack the zeal that was once so characteristic of ambassadors of Christ. How strange and almost out-of-place the immortal words of the faithful missionary, William Carey, seem today. Carey said, "Attempt great things for God, expect great things from God."

David Livingstone maintained a journal that lovingly recorded his experiences and trials as a pioneer missionary. This fascinating record reveals the long-term view that was prominent in all of his planning and enterprises. Livingstone states the following in his journal after ministering the Gospel to the chief of a remote village:

> A good and attentive audience, but immediately after the service I found the Chief had retired into a hut to drink beer.... A minister who had not seen so much pioneer service as I have done would have been shocked to see so little effect produced by an earnest discourse concerning the future judgment, but time must be given to allow the truth to sink into the dark mind and produce its effect. The earth shall be filled with the knowledge of the glory of the Lord—that is enough. We can afford to work in faith, for Omnipotence is pledged to fulfill the promise....
>
> A quiet audience today. The seed being sown, the least of all seeds now, but it will grow a mighty tree. It is as it were a small stone cut

out of a mountain, but it will fill the whole earth. He that believeth shall not make haste....

Missionaries in the midst of masses of heathenism seem like voices crying in the wilderness—Reformers before the Reformation. Future missionaries will see conversions follow every sermon. We prepare the way for them. May they not forget the pioneers who worked in the thick gloom with few rays to cheer, except such as flow from faith in God's promises! We work for a glorious future which we are not destined to see. We are only morning-stars shining in the dark, but the glorious morn will break....

When Livingstone was found by the natives, dead upon his knees, on May 4, 1873, it was a fitting end to a faith-filled life. He had died in the act of prayer, and who can doubt that the last prayer, like so many that preceded it, had borne up to God "this poor long downtrodden Africa"? Though his death occurred in an area where darkness and ignorance of God were universal, he had passed on with undiminished confidence in his testimony of former years: "Missionaries do not live before their time. Their great idea of converting the world to Christ is no phantom: it is Divine. Christianity will triumph. It is equal to all it has to perform."

May God grant His church a new army of missionaries that are equipped with the zeal and faith to dare great things for King Jesus.

Michael J. McHugh
Arlington Heights, Illinois
1999

— Contents —

Key Livingston in AFRICA

Atlantic Ocean

• Luanda

• Moçamedes

• Walvis

| 1000 Km |
| 1000 Mi. |

Cape

— Foreword —

D avid Livingstone was a faithful pioneer missionary whose greatest desire was granted only after his death: the cessation of the slave trade and the opening up of Africa to Christianity and lawful commerce.

Livingstone was brought up in a pious but poverty-stricken home in Scotland. He was an avid reader and borrowed extensively from the local library. By the age of nine, he had already committed to memory Psalm 119 and won a copy of the New Testament as a reward. When ten years old, David was employed fourteen hours a day, six days a week at the local cotton spinning factory. The young Livingstone managed to read in the factory by placing his book on a portion of the spinning jenny so that he could catch sentence after sentence as he passed at his work. He maintained a fairly constant study, undisturbed by the roar of the machinery.

His conversion at the age of twelve inspired him to resolve to devote his life to the alleviation of human misery. Three themes dominated his life: *evangelism, exploration,* and *emancipation.* He wrote at the time, "The salvation of men ought to be the chief desire and aim of every Christian." He therefore made a resolution that he would give to the cause of missions all that he might earn beyond what was required for his subsistence.

After ten years of daily drudgery at the cotton mill, David set out to study theology and medicine. Medical science in the 1830s was, by today's standards, primitive. Surgical operations were performed at hazardous speed because of the lack of anesthetics. Chloroform and ether were not introduced until several years later and the discovery of antiseptics lay twenty-five years ahead. The study of chemistry was growing, but physics had hardly started, and biochemistry and bacteriology were unknown. Nothing at all was known about the tropical diseases he was to encounter such as malaria and blackwater fever.

It was not in Livingstone's character to relax. He took his task and calling most seriously and whatever he did he performed thoroughly. He was uncompromising, diligent, and inflexible in his adherence to God's Word. Friends described him as "a man of resolute courage"; "fire, water, stonewall would not stop Livingstone in the fulfillment of any recognized duty."

When he landed in South Africa on March 17, 1841, David Livingstone was coming to a continent that was plagued with problems. Africa was still a place of mystery to the Europeans. The Arabs south of the Sahara never ventured inland far from the coast. The rivers were riddled with rapids and sand bars. The deadly malaria disease was widespread and inhibited travel. Entire expeditions of 300 to 400 men had been decimated by malaria. The African terrain was difficult to negotiate. Floods, tropical forests, and swamps thwarted wheeled transport.

Livingstone soon acquired a reputation for fearless faith—particularly when he walked to the Barka tribe who were infamous for the murder of four white traders whom they had mercilessly poisoned and strangled. As the first messenger of mercy in many regions, Livingstone soon received further challenge.

Chief Sechele pointed to the great Kalahari desert and declared, "You never can cross that country to the tribes beyond; it is utterly impossible even for us Black men." The challenge of crossing this obstacle began to fascinate Livingstone. Livingstone wrote: "I shall try to hold myself in readiness to go anywhere, provided it be forward." He described his three great daily challenges as *heat, harsh conditions,* and *hardness of hearts.* Thus he asserted:

> I hope to be permitted to work as long as I live beyond other men's line of things and plant the seed of the Gospel where others have not planted. But every excursion for that purpose will involve separation from my family for periods of four to five months. I am a missionary, heart and soul. God had an only Son, and He was a missionary and physician. A poor, poor imitation of Him I am, or wish to be. In His service I hope to live, in it I wish to die.

During his first missionary journey with his wife and children, their fourth child, Elizabeth, was born. Within a few weeks she had died and the rest of the family were sick. He received considerable undeserved criticism for the "irresponsibility" of taking a wife and four children on a missionary journey in the wilderness. Later, he was criticized for sending his family back to Britain while he pioneered the hinterland of Africa. When his wife rejoined him for his second great missionary expedition in the Zambezi Valley, she died of malaria. It was Livingstone who wrote,

> I shall open up a path into the interior or perish. May He bless us and make us blessings even unto death.... Shame upon us missionaries if we are to be outdone by slave traders! ... If Christian missionaries and Christian merchants could remain throughout the year in the interior of the continent, in ten years, slave dealers will be driven out of the market.

David Livingstone was inspired by an optimistic eschatology. Like most of the missionaries of the nineteenth century, Livingstone was a postmillenialist who held to the eschatology of victory. The optimistic missionary wrote,

> Discoveries and inventions are cumulative ... filling the earth with the glory of the Lord, all nations will sing His glory and bow before Him ... our work and its fruit are cumulative. We work towards a new state of things. Future missionaries will be rewarded by conversions for every sermon. We are their pioneers and helpers. Let them not forget the watchmen of the night, who worked when all was gloom and no evidence of success in the way of conversions cheers our path. They will doubtless have more light than we, but we serve our Master earnestly and proclaim the same Gospel as they will do.

Livingstone continued to persevere across the continent of Africa in the face of driving rains, chronic discomfort, rust, mildew and rot, while he became totally drenched, fatigued, and fever ridden. Hostile tribes demanded exorbitant payment for crossing their territory. Some tense moments were stared down by Livingstone, gun in hand. Trials tested the tenacity of the travel-wearied team. Meanwhile, the veteran missionary continued to ask, "Can the love of Christ not carry the missionary where the slave trade carries the traders?"

xii   David Livingstone, Man of Prayer and Action

After two years of pioneering across the hinterland of Africa, Livingstone reached Luanda. A ship called the *Forerunner* was ready to take him to England. Livingstone, however, chose to return overland to bring his guides and porters back to their village. Rather than risk their being sold into slavery in Portuguese West Africa, he preferred to take another two years crossing the continent that had almost killed him on his first journey! Had Livingstone chosen to return, however, he might well have ended his ministry. The ship sank with all hands lost (and with his journals)! Livingstone responded to this tragedy by asserting a simple childlike faith. He wrote,

> These privations, I beg you to observe, are not sacrifices. I think that word ought never to be mentioned in reference to anything we can do for Him who though He was rich, yet for our sakes became poor.

Often Livingstone endured excessive and unnecessary suffering and deprivation hacking through dense jungle on foot because lack of funds prevented him from affording the "luxury" of a canoe!

Livingstone often saw the sickening sight of the Islamic slave trade; Livingstone's mere presence often sent the Yao slave raiders scurrying into the bushes. Many hundreds of slaves were set free by Livingstone and his coworkers. On one occasion, a war party of Yao warriors attacked the missionary party. While attempting to avoid confrontation, the team found themselves cut off and surrounded by the aggressive and bloodthirsty mob. Finally, Livingstone was forced to give the command to return fire. The slave traders fled. These incidents led to much criticism in England. Charles Livingstone, his brother, on hearing one outburst from Britain replied:

> If you were in Africa and saw a host of murderous savages aiming their heavily laden muskets and poisoned arrows at you, more light might enter your mind ... and if it didn't, great daylight would enter your body through arrow and bullet holes!

It was Livingstone's great desire to see the slave trade cease. First, there was the internal slave trade between hostile tribes. Secondly, there were slave traders from the coast, Arabs or Portuguese, for whom local tribes were encouraged to collect slaves by force. Thirdly, there were the parties sent out from Portuguese and Arab coastal towns with cloths, beads, muskets, and ammunition to exchange for slaves.

Livingstone had the grace to see that his mission was part of a divine plan to set many souls free from slavery, both physical and spiritual. Livingstone's great goal of bringing to the world's attention the plight of the Islamic slave trade in Africa was achieved largely through the work of his convert, American journalist Henry Morton Stanley.

The challenge of Livingstone rings out to us today:

> Can that be called a sacrifice which is simply paid back as a small part of the great debt owing to our God, which we can never repay … it is emphatically no sacrifice. Say rather, it is a privilege!

> I beg to direct your attention to Africa: I know that in a few years I shall be cut off from that country, which is now open; do not let it be shut again! I go back to Africa to try to make an open path for commerce and Christianity: will you carry out the work which I have begun? I leave it with you!

Dr. Peter Hammond
Director, Frontline Fellowship
Cape Town, South Africa
May 1, 1999

During the days of his youth, David Livingstone came
to the most significant decision of his life.
He decided to offer himself to one
of the missionary societies
for foreign service.

CHAPTER 1

Days of His Youth

1813–1840

The year 1813 in which my story opens was a momentous one in the history of Europe. The French Emperor Napoleon was seeking to dominate Europe. Although Napoleon was the victor at Lutzen and Bautzen, he had been defeated at Leipzig, on one of the bloodiest battlefields in modern warfare. Away in the Pyrenees Mountains, however, British general Wellington was grappling with Soult and, step by step, driving him back on to French soil. Among those who were fighting in the ranks of the British army were at least two men bearing the name of Livingstone. It is doubtful whether they even heard, amid the excitement and peril of the time, that away in peaceful Scotland, and in their brother Neil's home, a lad had been born in Blantyre and christened by the good and Scriptural name of David. Yet it may come to be believed some day that the birth of David Livingstone may well have been of more vital influence upon the future of the world than even the battle of Waterloo in which Napoleon's star was set in blood two years later. For to open up a continent and lead the way in the Christianization of its countless millions was one of the "more renowned" victories for peace in the history of the world, and vastly superior to overthrowing one form of military domination in Europe.

The family of Livingstones or Livingstons—for David Livingstone himself spelled his name for many years without the final "e"—came from the Island of Ulva off the coast of Argyllshire, Scotland. Not much of interest is known about them except that one of them died at Culloden fighting for the Stuarts; so that the "fighting blood" in their veins had its way with them before David's more immediate kinsmen crossed the seas to the Peninsula. The most distinguished member of the family, David Livingstone, inherited the Highlander's daring and love of exploits combined with the most patient spirit, and left behind him an unstained record as an explorer and faithful missionary of Jesus Christ. Towards the close of the eighteenth century his grandfather had crossed from Ulva and settled in Blantyre, a Scottish village on the Clyde that had certainly no romantic attraction. He was employed in a cotton factory there. Most of his sons went off to the wars; but one of them, Neil, settled in Blantyre as a dealer in tea. He had been previously apprenticed to David Hunter, a tailor. And, as many a good apprentice has done before him, married his master's daughter. Neil Livingstone and his brave wife had a hard fight of it to make a living out of a small tea business, and to educate and rear their children. Two of the children died in infancy, but three sons and two daughters grew up in that humble home. David was the second son. He was born on March 19, 1813.

The small struggling tradesman who was the father of David Livingstone has had little justice done to him either by the novelist or by historians. He is usually represented as a man who could not afford to support a soul, and whose interests are limited to sordid and petty transactions across a counter, not always nor often of a scrupulous and honorable character. The reputation is very ill-deserved. The small shop has proved itself as good a training ground as any other for scholars, saints, and heroes; and, but for the fact that our prejudices die hard, we should recognize that it is so. Neil Livingstone and his wife may have lived a narrow life, serving faithfully their customers and dividing their interests between their family, their business, and the little Independent Chapel where Neil Livingstone was a deacon. Nevertheless, they found their sphere large enough for the practice of the fundamental Christian virtues, as well as for the noblest of all interests—the interest in the progress of the Kingdom of God throughout the world. This was one family tradition of which David Livingstone was immensely proud.

A saying had come down to them attributed to an ancestor that in all the family history there was no record of any dishonest man. When Deacon Neil Livingstone and his wife had passed away, the epitaph on their grave recorded the gratitude of their children for "poor and honest parents." In this simple and public fashion, they expressed their thanks for the honesty of one who, when he sold a pound of tea, gave neither short weight, nor an inferior product. They also gave thanks for the poverty of their parents, recognizing in poverty one of those hard but kind necessities that make for industry and courage and patience; and that the children of the poor commonly leave the world their debtor for serviceable activities than the children of the well-to-do, who have less spur to their ambitions. It was eminently characteristic of David Livingstone that he should thus avow his thanks for the honesty and poverty of his father and mother.

The mother of David Livingstone was a woman of great charm and force of character—a delicate little woman with a wonderful flow of Christian joy. In her, rare devoutness and sterling common sense were combined. She was a careful and thrifty homemaker who had to make every sixpence go as far as possible; but she was remembered for her unfailing cheerfulness and serenity, and there was always something to be saved out of the meager income when the work of the local church needed extra support. She came from a Christian family, and her father, David Hunter, was a tailor. He received his first religious impressions at an open-air service, held while the snow was falling fast, and used to tell that so absorbed was he in the realization of the truth of the Gospel, that, though before the end of the sermon the snow was ankle-deep, he had no sensation of cold. He lived to be eighty-seven, was a prolific reader, bore severe trials with unflinching courage, and earned the high respect of the countryside.

It is impossible to exaggerate what David Livingstone owed to the stock from which he sprang and the bracing influences of his early environment. Although David's home education was generally very sound and beneficial, it did have one weakness. It seems that the Deacon had forbidden his son to read science fiction novels and books of general science. So far as novels are concerned, the harm done was probably slight; for no one is well read in the Bible and the *Pilgrim's Progress* without receiving a proper education, and a sufficient cultivation of his imagination; while history, biography, books of travel, and missionary records amply served the same purpose. Nevertheless, the omission of books of science was an evidence of the old foolish notion that there is an essential antagonism between science and religion. This assumption came near to doing David permanent harm. His religious difficulties did not disappear until in his own words "having lighted on those admirable works of Dr. Thomas Dick, *The Philosophy of Religion*, and *The Philosophy of a Future State*, it was gratifying to find that he had enforced my own conviction that religion and science were friendly to one another." Few people in the nineteenth century were destined to do more towards the practical reconciliation of science and religion than David Livingstone.

> Livingstone was a born naturalist, and despite his father's ill-advised prejudices, he made himself a scientist at a very early age, searching old quarries for the shells in the limestone permeated with carbon, scouring Clydeside for "samples," and arranging the flora of the district in botanical order. These expeditions were often very prolonged, and involved the endurance of fatigue and hunger…
> Unconsciously he was bracing himself physically for the toils and tasks of later years.

It is interesting to find that even in his very young days he had a mind and will of his own, and that not even the love and respect he felt for his father could shake his own conviction of truth. The last time his father "applied the rod" was when David refused to read Wilberforce's *Practical Christianity*. The boy thought the matter over in his canny Scottish way and concluded that, on the whole, the rod was the less severe form of punishment. So he took the rod and refused a religious book for which he had no use. Looking back upon his own religious development in later years, he used to confess that at this stage he was "color-blind." When he was led to see that God and Nature are "not at strife," and that God does not say one thing to the theologian and its contrary to the scientist, he accepted in his own simple and sincere way the Christian Gospel, and drew from it the same splendid faith in the universality of the Kingdom of God that inspired the souls of the first apostles. To David Livingstone, to become a Christian was to become in spirit and desire a missionary. It is only necessary to add that the faith which he accepted with the full consent of heart and mind as a lad in Blantyre was the faith in which he died.

The days of David Livingstone's boyhood were great days for missions. The churches were everywhere awakening to their opportunity and responsibility to fulfill the Great Commission given by Christ. Letters from remote parts of the world, where the ancient battle between Christ and heathenism was being fought out anew, were eagerly read and deeply pondered by God's people. The romance and heroism of the majestic campaign captured and kindled both young and old. The year of Livingstone's birth was a year of singular triumph in the South Seas. It was the year when his great countryman, Robert Morrison, completed his translation of the New Testament into Chinese. When he was some six or seven years old, another famous Scottish missionary, Robert Moffat, was settling on the Kuruman; and Mrs. Moffat bore in her arms a baby girl destined to become David Livingstone's wife. The life of Henry Martyn was a supreme call to consecration, while the story of the heroes and heroines of the Moravian missions was almost as familiar in that humble Scottish home as the history of the Apostle Paul.

An especially powerful influence in moving Livingstone to his life decision was the appeal of Charles Gutzlaff for medical missionaries for China.

Livingstone was a born naturalist, and despite his father's ill-advised prejudices, he made himself a scientist at a very early age, searching old quarries for the shells in the limestone permeated with carbon, scouring Clydeside for "samples," and arranging the flora of the district in botanical order. These expeditions were often very prolonged, and involved the endurance of fatigue and hunger, but the lad could not be discouraged. Unconsciously he was bracing himself physically for the toils and tasks of later years. There is a fine story about the revenge he took upon his native African escort, on one occasion, who had been misguided enough to talk disrespectfully about his slim figure and shortness of stature. Thereupon, Livingstone took them along for two or three days at the top of their speed till they cried out for mercy! He had not scoured Clydeside for samples for nothing. His fearlessness is well illustrated in his daring and reckless exploit of climbing the ruins of Bothwell Castle, so that he might carve his name higher than any other boy had carved his. There, too, was the childlike ambition, which remained with him to the end, to do something which nobody else could surpass. "No one," he wrote at the very end of his life, on his last expedition, "will cut me out after this exploration is accomplished." Then he adds finely, "and may the good Lord of all help me to show myself one of His stouthearted servants, an honor to my children, and perhaps to my country and race." The story of Livingstone is told there: it is the story of one of the good Lord's stout-hearted servants.

All the drudgery and hardship of his lot went to make him the man he was. The days of his boyhood were "the good old days"—the days when ten-year-old children were sent to work in the factories, and David went with the rest. He worked from six o'clock in the morning till eight o'clock at night, and many people have heard how he used to place the book he was studying on a portion of the spinning jenny, and snatch a sentence or two as he passed at his work. He tells us he thus kept "a pretty constant study, undisturbed by the roar of machinery," and that this habit of concentration stood him in good stead in later years when he wanted to read and write even "amidst the dancing and song of savages." As if this were not enough, after a fourteen-hour day in the factory he would go off to a night school provided by the employers and then home to work at his Latin till "mother put out the candle." It is well for ten-year-old humanity when it has a mother to put out the candle, or young David might have worked himself to death, and where would Africa have been then?

Nine years of such severe and determined work as this brought him to college age. Glasgow University was close by, and as he was promoted by this time and able to earn enough in the summer to keep him during the other six months, he entered as a student majoring in Greek and medicine. The Scottish universities were a paradise for poor and struggling students who had more brains and character than money, but the education was not free in those days. The money for fees had to be pinched and scraped, but it was found somehow, and in the early winter of 1836, David and his father walked to the city from Blantyre and trudged the streets of Glasgow all day, with the snow upon the ground, till at last they found a room in "Rotten Row" that could be rented for two shillings a week. Lodged thus as cheaply as could be managed, he applied himself with all his unfailing diligence and zest to learn Greek and medicine, as well as to such theological studies as could be undertaken under the leadership of the Rev. Dr. Wardlaw—one of Glasgow's most famous divines—who trained men for the Congregational ministry, and for whom Livingstone had a great admiration.

During his second session at Glasgow (1837–1838,) David Livingstone came to the most significant decision of his life. He decided to offer himself to one of the missionary societies for foreign service. He chose the London Missionary Society because of his sympathy with the nondenominational structure of its basis. It existed "to send neither Episcopacy, nor Presbyterianism, nor Independency to the heathen, but the Gospel of Christ." "This," said Livingstone "exactly agreed with my ideas." He was a member of a Congregational church, and the London Missionary Society had always been in the main supported by these churches. Nevertheless, the Society was founded by Evangelical churchmen and prominent Presbyterians, as well as by Congregationalists, and nothing appealed more to Livingstone than this union of Christian people in the service of an unchristian world.

In due course the acceptance of his offer arrived, and in the early autumn of 1838, he traveled to London where he was to appear before the Mission Board at 57 Aldersgate Street. One can imagine that—apart from the momentous character of his visit and the anxiety he must have felt at the acceptance by the Directors— this first visit to London must have been a most impressive one to the young Scotsman. He heard many distinguished preachers and visited the famous sites of London. Among other places, he went with a companion to Westminster Abbey. It is a thrilling thought that he was never known to enter that Abbey again until his remains were borne there amid the lamentations of the whole civilized world.

The examination by the Directors was satisfactory, and according to the custom of the time, Livingstone was committed for a short period of probation to the tutorship of the Rev. Richard Cecil, the minister of the little town of Chipping Ongar in Essex. There he was expected to give evidence of his ability to commence a preaching ministry. He was sent one Sunday evening to preach in the village of Stanford Rivers, where the tradition of Livingstone's first effort at preaching is still cherished. The raw, somewhat heavy-looking Scottish youth, to whom public speech was always a difficulty, gave out his text "very deliberately." That was all the congregation got. The sermon composed on the text had fled, owing to the nervous embarrassment produced by a handful of people in a village chapel. "Friends," said the youth, "I have forgotten all I had to say"— and "hurrying out of the pulpit" he left the chapel. I have no doubt that *hurrying* is the right word. Never was failure more absolute. It is hardly to be wondered at that the Rev. Richard Cecil reported to the Directors his fears that Livingstone had mistaken his vocation. It was a risk to send someone to preach to the heathen who might possibly forget what he had come to say when he arrived. Moreover, criticism was made of his extreme slowness and hesitancy in prayer. Yet the man who was nearly rejected by the Society on this account, died on his knees in the heart of Africa while all the world was awed by the thought that David Livingstone passed away in the act of prayer. As it was, his probation was extended, and at the end of another two months he was finally accepted, and went up to London to continue his medical studies in the London Hospitals. One of the most striking things ever written about him was by the celebrated Dr. Isaac Taylor, of Ongar. "Now after nearly forty years," he writes, "I remember his step, the characteristic forward tread, firm, simple, resolute, neither fast nor slow, no hurry and no dawdle, but which evidently meant—getting there!" In November 1840, he was able to return to Glasgow and qualify as a Licentiate of the Faculty of Physicians and Surgeons, and a few days later, he said good-bye to the old folks at home, one of whom—his father—he was never to see on earth again.

On November twentieth, he was ordained at Albion Chapel, London, and three weeks later he sailed on the *George* to Algoa Bay in South Africa. One chapter in his memorable life was now definitely closed. Among the memories in it, there are few if any that he cherished more than that of his old Sunday School teacher, David Hogg, who sent for him as he lay dying and said, "Now lad, make religion the everyday business of your life and not a thing of fits and starts, for if you do, temptation and other things will not get the better of you." It is hardly too much to say that the old man's deathbed counsel became the watchword of young David's life.

Looking back upon it now, it is easy to believe that it was not
God's will that Livingstone should spend his life in the work of
a missionary settlement, but should be driven out along the
lonely, adventurous path where his calling lay.

Chapter 2

God's Call to Africa

1841–1852

A voyage of five months saw Livingstone at Algoa Bay, preparing for his first journey into the interior of Africa—"the grave of so many" but the continent of his renown. Few people realize that up until a short time before his departure from London he had hoped and intended to go to China as a medical missionary. Nevertheless, the "Opium War" was still in progress, and for the time being China was impossible. Moreover, Livingstone was brought under the influence of one of the greatest personalities in modern missionary enterprise. Robert Moffat was home on furlough, and his wonderful story no less than his striking presence exerted an influence over the young Scot and changed the goal of his ambition. Dr. Moffat often described the numberless African villages stretching away to the north where no missionary had yet penetrated, and his appeal found a ready response in Livingstone's heart.

It was to Dr. Moffat's station at Kuruman that David Livingstone took his first journey. The distance was seven hundred miles, and he immediately surrendered to the interest and delight of travel by ox wagon, the freedom of the open air life, the variety of the scenery and sport, and the attractiveness of the natives who engaged his sympathy from the first. It was now that his hardy training in Scotland stood him in good stead. He knew how to put up with inconveniences cheerfully and face difficulties with resolution, while his resourcefulness was as inexhaustible as his kindliness. That "characteristic forward tread" of which the famous missionary Isaac Taylor had spoken which "meant getting there," was put to the proof and not found wanting. To him there was a God-ordained way out of every situation, however critical, and the "bold free course" which he took with the natives, together with his medical skill and unwearied goodness, won their loyalty. They recognized him as a great chief, and his whole career is eloquent of the extraordinary devotion which he inspired in them.

At the end of May 1841, he was at Kuruman, with instructions from the directors of the Society to turn his attention to the North—instructions that absolutely coincided with his own aspiration. It is notable that he formed the very highest opinion of the value of Christian missions from the results that he saw. Let it be remembered that he was always a slow, cautious Scot in all his judgments, with a severely truthful and scientific mind, and his testimony becomes the more valuable. "Everything I witnessed surpassed my hopes," he writes home; "if this is a fair sample, the statements of the missionaries, as to their success, are far within the mark." He is full of the praises of the Christian Hottentots, who are "far superior in attainments to what I had expected"—their worship reminded him of the old covenanters. It was thus, then, that with his zeal for his mission of evangelism greatly stimulated, he started north to the country of the Bakwains.

> "If we wait till there is no danger," said Livingstone, "we shall never go at all."

A number of problems arose, however, that caused Livingstone to return to Kuruman to plan a better campaign. The first step was a characteristic one. It was to isolate himself absolutely from all European society and live among the natives, so as to learn their language and study their habits and their laws. For six months, he rigorously pursued his plan and found his reward in the new appreciation he gained of the native character and mode of thinking, and the extent to which he conquered their confidences. So far advanced had he become in the knowledge of their language that he was able to enjoy a laugh at himself for "turning poet." One can believe that for Livingstone, this was no easy work, but he succeeded in making Sechuana translations of several hymns which were afterwards adopted and printed by the French missionaries. "If they had been bad," he says in his naive way, "I don't see that they can have had any motive for using them."

He was waiting now for the final decision of the directors authorizing the advance into the unoccupied district of the north. The decision was long in coming. We must recognize that such a resolution was not an easy one for those who carried all the responsibilities at home. Even their most trusted advisers on the actual field were not agreed. Dr. Philip, the special representative of the Society at the Cape, and a man of great personal power and sagacity, shook his head over Livingstone's impetuosity and talked about the dangers. "If we wait till there is no danger," said Livingstone, "we shall never go at all." It was quite true, but there were big problems of policy to be decided. Settlements for educational and industrial developments had proved their value. On the other hand, Livingstone had unanswerable logic on his side when he argued that the missionaries in the South had too scanty a population and that the call to possess the North was urgent, for the traders and the slavers were penetrating there, and the gospel of Christ was imperatively needed.

There was a long delay, but in the meantime Livingstone was making proof of his ministry. His medical knowledge helped to spread his fame. He fought the rainmakers at their own arts with the scientific weapon of irrigation and won his battle. He made friends with the Bechuana chief, Sechéle, one of the most intelligent and interesting of the many great natives who surrendered to the charm of Livingstone. Sechéle was deeply impressed by the missionary's message, but profoundly troubled in spirit. He said, "You startle me—these words make all my bones to shake—I have no more strength in me. Nevertheless, my forefathers were living at the same time yours were, and how is it that they did not send them word about these terrible things sooner. They all passed away into darkness without knowing whither they were going." When Livingstone tried to explain to him the gradual spread of the Gospel knowledge, the chief refused to believe that the whole earth could be visited. There was a barrier at his very door—the Kalahari desert. Nobody could cross it. Even those who knew the country would perish, and no missionary would have an opportunity to bring God's Word. As for his own people there was no difficulty in converting them, Sechéle reasoned, always assuming that Livingstone would go to work in the right way. "Do you imagine these people will ever believe by your merely talking to them? I can make them do nothing except by thrashing them, and if you like, I will call my headmen and with our *litupa* (whips of rhinoceros hide) we will soon make them all believe together." It must be confessed, however, that Sechéle's state-church principles did not commend themselves to the mind of an ardent proponent of human liberty like Livingstone. "In our relations with the people," he writes, "we were simply strangers exercising no authority or control whatever. Our influence depended entirely on persuasion, and having taught them by kind conversation as well as by public instruction, I expected them to do what their own sense of right and wrong dictated." He then sets on record "five instances in which, by our influence on public opinion, war was prevented" and pays a high tribute to the intelligence of the natives who in many respects excel "our own uneducated peasantry." This attitude of appreciation and respectful sympathy was the secret of Livingstone's unparalleled influence over the African tribes.

It was on a return from a visit to Sechéle in June 1843 that Livingstone heard the good news of the formal sanction of the forward movement. He hailed the decision, as he said, "with inexpressible delight" and, in a fine letter written to Mr. Cecil, declared his fixed resolve to give less attention to the art of physical healing and more to spiritual "healing." He has no ambition to be "a very good doctor but a useless drone of a missionary." He feels that to carry out this purpose will involve some self-denial, but he will make the sacrifice cheerfully. As for the charge of ambition, "I really am ambitious to preach beyond other men's lines.... I am only determined to go on and do all I can, while able, for the poor degraded people of the North."

In less than two months, he was ready for the new move. The first journey was two hundred miles to the northeast, to Mabotsa, which he had previously noted as suitable for a station. Here he built a house with his own hands and settled down for three years' work among the Bakatlas. During this period, two events occurred that were especially notable. The first event almost ended his career. The facts are well-known from Livingstone's own graphic but simple description. He had gone with the Bakatlas to hunt some lions which had committed serious disruptions in the village. The lions were encircled by the natives but broke through the line and escaped. As Livingstone was returning, however, he saw one of the beasts on a small hill, and fired into him at about thirty yards' distance. Loading again, he heard a shout, and "looking half-round saw the lion just in the act of springing upon me." The lion seized him by the shoulder and "growling horribly close

to my ear, he shook me as a terrier dog does a rat." We now see the advantage of a scientific education. Livingstone was able to analyze his own feelings and emotions during the process of being gnawed by a lion. He observed that "the shock produced a stupor, a sort of dreaminess"; there was "no sense of pain, nor feeling of terror." He compares it to the influence of chloroform and argues that "this peculiar state is probably produced in all humans and animals killed by the carnivora and, if so, is a merciful provision by our benevolent Creator for lessening the pain of death." So interesting does

Livingstone find these observations, that it seems as if he must have been almost disappointed when the lion released him and turned his attention to others less well equipped for scientific investigation. On the whole, Livingstone escaped marvelously well, but the shoulder bone was crunched into splinters, and there were eleven teeth wounds on the upper part of his arm. The arm indeed was never really well again. It will be remembered that it was by the false joint in this limb that the remains of Livingstone were identified on their arrival in England. It will also be remembered that, as has been so well said, "for thirty years afterwards all his labors and adventures, entailing such exertion and fatigue, were undertaken with a limb so maimed that it was painful for him to raise a rifle or, in fact, to place the left arm in any position above the level of the shoulder."

This was a difficult trial indeed, but Providence has a way of making up to good men for afflictions of this kind. Livingstone's compensation came to him in the following year, when he had something to face that demanded more daring than a mere everyday encounter with lions. He had been a bachelor in Africa for four years, and he had resolved to try his fortune with Mary Moffat, Dr. Moffat's eldest daughter. The proposal was made "beneath one of the fruit trees" at Kuruman in 1844. He got the answer he desired and deserved, and Mary Moffat took him with all his erratic ways and became his devoted wife. "She was always the best spoke in the wheel at home," he writes, "and when I took her with me on two occasions to Lake Ngami, and far beyond, she endured more than some who have written large books of travels." In course of time, three sons and a daughter came to "cheer their solitude" and increase their responsibilities. From the first, however, they set themselves to fulfill what Livingstone called the ideal missionary life— "the husband, a jack-of-all-trades, and the wife, a maid-of-all-work." The catalog of necessary skills in the routine of an African missionary sounds somewhat embarrassing, and one realizes that the ordinary college training is in many respects incomplete. Here it is, as Livingstone expressed it—"Building, gardening, cobbling, doctoring, tinkering, carpentering, gun-mending, farriering,[1] wagon-mending, preaching, schooling, lecturing on physics, occupying a chair

---

[1] The shoeing of horses done by a farrier, i.e., a blacksmith; farrier sometimes refers to one who treats the diseases of horses.

in divinity, and helping my wife to make soap, candles, and clothes."
It was certainly a busy and challenging career. He was carrying the
whole of his world upon his own broad shoulders, and was guide,
philosopher, and friend to a vast district.

He had his enemies, too, as those who champion the rights of
the poor and helpless are sure to have. To the North were to be
found settlements of unscrupulous and marauding
Boers—descendants of
Dutch Calvinist and French
Huguenot colonists; they
held by all the unenlightened
views of the relation of the
white races to the black,
which were only recently extinct in England where the
financial interest in slavery
died hard in 1833. These
Boer marauders lived largely
on slave labor and on pillage,
and Livingstone was brought
into open conflict with

> Livingstone
> had unanswerable
> logic on his side when he
> argued that the missionaries
> in the South had too scanty a
> population and that the call to
> possess the North was urgent,
> for the traders and the slavers
> were penetrating there, and
> the gospel of Christ was
> imperatively needed.

them. On one side, they may be said to have barred his advance.
The tribes he served and loved lived under the cloud of a Boer invasion. The time was to come when the cloud would burst over Chief
Sechéle and his unoffending people, when his wives would be slain
and his children carried away into slavery, when many of the bravest of his people would be massacred, and Livingstone's house sacked
and gutted in his absence. This complicity of the northern Boers in
those outrages on native tribes—which history most frequently associates with the Portuguese in Africa—earned Livingstone's stern
indignation. Even though Livingstone detested slavery, he never did
the Boers of South Africa the injustice of confounding the lawless
raiders with the main body of settlers, of whom he respectfully wrote,
"the Boers generally ... are a sober, industrious, and most hospitable body of peasantry."

He had, however, already begun to have glimpses of what his life-witness was to be. He saw that the curse of Africa lay not only in the internal conflicts of tribe with tribe. That form of misery was original to the continent and its unchristian inhabitants; but a new curse had fallen upon the unhappy people by the intrusion of those who united with a higher material civilization to produce a more developed and refined form of cruelty. The diabolical cunning and callousness that, under the guise of trading, would gain the confidence of a peaceful tribe, only at last to rise up some fatal night, murder the old, enslave the young, burn the huts, and march the chained gang hundreds of miles to the sea, have made the records of African slavery the most awful reading in human history. Imagination carries the story one step further. We hardly need a genius to suggest to us the horror of a slave ship under the torrid tropical skies, with its dead and dying human freight. When the slave trade is realized in all its accumulated horrors, it is easy to understand how, to a man of Livingstone's noble Christian sensibility, the manifest duty of the Church of Christ was to engage in a war-to-the-death struggle against this darkest of all inhumanities.

He was planning his campaign during the years when he passed with his wife and children from one settlement to another. Three houses he built with his own hands and made some progress in the cultivation of gardens round them. The first was at Mabotsa. It was the home to which he brought his young bride, and to leave it went to his heart. His going was the result of the attitude adopted towards him by a brother missionary. Sooner than cause scandal among the tribe, he resolved to give everything up and go elsewhere. "Paradise will make amends for all our privations and sorrows here," he says simply. It is something to know that the missionary who did him this injustice lived "to manifest a very different spirit."

Livingstone next cast in his lot with Sechéle and his people, and built his second house at Chonuane, some forty miles from Mabotsa. It was hard work, and it made a big drain on his very small income, but it was not his way to complain. The hardship fell more severely on his wife and infant children, and he felt sad to know that they were inconvenienced. The house was finished sometime later, and a school was erected too, where the children were instructed and services held, but the harsh climate was against a long settlement at Chonuane. A period of prolonged drought set in. Supplies were exhausted. The people had to go further afield, and the position became untenable. There was nothing for the Livingstones to do but leave. All the labor of rebuilding had to be undertaken again, this time at Kolobeng, another forty miles on. Providence was indeed to Livingstone "like as an eagle stirring up the nest." Such of the tribe as were left went with him and a new village was constructed. Livingstone and his family lived for a year in "a mere hut."

In 1848 the new house was actually built, despite some serious personal accidents of which he made light in his usual way. "What a mercy to be in a house again!" he writes home. "A year in a little hut through which the wind blew our candles into glorious icicles (as a poet would say) by night, and in which crowds of flies continually settled on the eyes of our poor little children by day, makes us value our present castle. Oh Janet, know thou, if thou art given to building castles in the air, that that is easy work compared to erecting cottages on the ground!" Such was the building of his third house, the one that was afterwards sacked by a small band of Boers. Then he built no more houses. Indeed, he never had a home of his own in Africa afterwards. The dark problem of Central Africa had him in its grip. In 1852, he sent his wife and children home to England, and he himself became like that Son of Man whose example he followed so nearly, one "who had no where to lay his head."

Before that time came, however, he had laid the foundation of his fame as an explorer by crossing the Kalahari Desert and discovering Lake Ngami in the late 1840s. The circumstances that gave rise to this journey are easily detailed. The drought continued at Kolobeng as pitilessly as at Chonuane. Only the power of Livingstone's personality sufficed to retain the faith and loyalty of the tribes. He writes that they were always treated with "respectful kindness" and never had an enemy among the natives. His enemies were among the "dirty whites," who knew that he was the most dangerous obstacle to the slave raids, and who objected to his policy of training Christian native teachers to be evangelists among their own kinfolk. But though the tribes remained loyal, the fact remained that Livingstone had led a migration which had not resulted in a permanent settlement; neither could he command the rain as their own rainmakers professed to be able to do. The heathen superstition that hostile doctors had put their country under an evil charm so that no rain should fall on it, prevailed even against their faith in the missionary. Sechéle's more enlightened mind found it difficult to understand why Livingstone's God did not answer the prayer for rain. Yet the work went forward at Kolobeng.

The chief Sechéle, after long hesitation on Livingstone's part, was baptized and entered into communion with the little church. Trouble followed when he "went home, gave each of his superfluous wives new clothing, and all his own goods, which they had been accustomed to keep in their huts for him, and sent them to their parents with an intimation that he had no fault to find with them, but that in parting with them he wished to follow the will of God." It was his solution to the problem of multiple wives that can never be satisfactorily solved, and it was both courageous and generous, but the result was seen in the fiercer resentment of the relatives of the women; and while little or none of this fell upon Livingstone, it served seriously to prejudice the religion which was responsible for Sechéle's action.

On every count, it was desirable to find the new and permanent station, where that central training-ground for native missionaries could be established which Livingstone had constantly in view, and where the water supply would be less likely to fail. But where to go? In the south, the field was well supplied with missionaries. To the east were the unfriendly Dutch Boers, bent on making mischief. To the north lay the Kalahari desert, which Sechéle had pronounced to be an impassable barrier to the progress of Christianity. "It is utterly impossible even to us black men," he had said. But the word "impossible" was not in Livingstone's dictionary.

If my readers will take the trouble to look at an old map of South Africa they will find the whole vast track of the west which lies to the north of the Orange River and includes Bechuana Land and Damara Land, described as desert, and the Kalahari desert in the eastern portion of it. Kolobeng lay at the extreme west of what we know today as the Transvaal, some two hundred and fifty miles from Pretoria, and was more than four thousand feet above sea level, near the sources of the Limpopo River, which flows north and east, until it finally joins the ocean at Delagoa Bay. A straight line to Lake Ngami would have taken the travelers in a northwesterly direction a distance of little more than three hundred miles. But it is doubtful whether they could have survived such a journey across an untrodden route, even if they had known accurately where the great lake lay. They were certainly well inspired to go due north to the Zouga River, and then follow it westward to the lake, though this route must have added two hundred miles to their journey. Three other Europeans, Colonel Steele, Mr. Murray, and Mr. Oswell— the latter, one of Livingstone's lifelong friends and a mighty African hunter—joined the expedition, which started on June 1, 1849, and reached the lake on August 1. Livingstone has given us a most graphic and detailed description of the desert with its sandy soil, its *wadies* (dry river beds, except during periods of rainfall), its trackless plains, its prairie grass, its patches of bush, and the singular products of its soil with roots like large turnips that hold fluid beneath the soil. Above all Livingstone noted the desert watermelons on which the Bushmen as well as the elephants, antelopes, and even lions and hyenas subsist. He found the Bushmen to be a thin, wiry, merry race capable of great endurance, as indeed the denizens of the desert must be. They existed under conditions that inspired the Bechuana with terror, for, to add to the other dangers, the desert was at times infested with serpents.

It was a hazardous enterprise to which Livingstone and his fellow travelers were committed, and, humanly speaking, its success depended wholly on the discovery of water at periodic intervals. The "caravan" was a considerable one. Eighty cattle and twenty horses were not deemed too many for the wagons and for riding; these had to be watered, and the twenty men besides. Progress was necessarily slow. None could face the burning heat of the midday hours. They had to move forward in the mornings and evenings. The wagon wheels sank deep into the soft, hot sand; and the poor oxen dragging them laboriously forward were, at a critical time, nearly four days without water, "and their masters scarcely better off." Aided, however, by the experience and keen instinct of the natives, they found wells in unsuspected places, and eventually made the banks of the Zouga River. After that, progress was easy. Leaving the wagons and oxen, they took to canoes, or snaked their way along the river banks, until, on the morning of August first, they found themselves gazing on the waters of Lake Ngami, the first white people to see it, so far as they knew.

It had been one of the goals of Livingstone for the journey that he would meet the famous chief Sebituane, who had saved the life of Sechéle in his infancy, and who was renowned as a warrior and as a powerful and intelligent ruler. It meant another two hundred miles of travel to the north, and the jealousies of the chiefs and their real or assumed fears for Livingstone's safety, prevented the realization of his hopes on this journey. There was nothing for it but to go back to Kolobeng, where the drought persisted as absolute as ever.

Livingstone's congregation and Mrs. Livingstone's school had disappeared in search of better watered lands. It was clear that for Livingstone there was "no abiding city" here. He resolved to transport his wife and three children to the north. He made more of an eastward circuit this time, and Sechéle accompanied them to the fords of the Zouga. Mrs. Livingstone was the first white lady to see Lake Ngami, but the purposed visit to Sebituane was again to be deferred.

Livingstone's aid was invoked for a fever-stricken party of Englishmen who were hunting ivory. One was already dead, but the others recovered under his treatment. His own children, however, sickened, and the party had to retire to "the pure air of the desert," and so home to Kolobeng where another child was born to them, only to be carried away by an epidemic. The infant's name was Elizabeth.

"Here is the first grave in all that country," writes the bereaved father, "marked as the resting-place of one of whom it is believed and confessed that she shall live again."

After a visit to Kuruman to rest and recruit, they were ready in April 1851 for a third attempt to reach Sebituane. Mr. Oswell, the most valuable of comrades, was again with them. The journey was successful, but it came dangerously near to being disastrous to the whole family. This crisis occurred on the far side of the Zouga River, as they were traveling northward across absolute desert. The Bushman guide lost his way, and the supply of water in the wagons had been wasted by one of the servants. Livingstone tells the incident in a single paragraph, but the agony of it must nearly have killed him and his wife. "The next morning, the less there was of water the more thirsty the little rogues became. The idea of their perishing before our eyes was terrible. It would almost have been a relief to me to have been reproached with being the entire cause of the catastrophe, but not one syllable of upbraiding was uttered by their mother, though the tearful eye told the agony within. In the afternoon of the fifth day, to our inexpressible relief, some of the men returned with a supply of that fluid of which we had never before felt the true value." At last the often-postponed pleasure of meeting and greeting Sebituane was fulfilled, and the famous chief more than justified all expectations. He met the party on the Chobe River and conducted them with great ceremony and hospitality to his home. The way seemed to be opening for a new and auspicious missionary settlement, when in a few days Sebituane sickened and died. It was one of the greatest blows which Livingstone ever experienced. Its tragic suddenness almost stunned him. Looking back upon it now, it is easy to believe that it was not God's will that Livingstone should spend his life in the work of a missionary settlement, but should be driven out along the lonely, adventurous path where his calling lay.

But at the moment he only felt severely the crushing of his hopes and frustration of his plans. Sebituane's daughter, who succeeded to the chieftainship, was full of kindly promise, but difficulties multiplied in the way of a settlement, which further exploration of the district did not diminish. Penetrating a hundred and thirty miles to the north, Oswell and Livingstone came upon the broad channel of a noble river, called by the natives the Seshsome, three hundred yards wide even there, more than a thousand miles from the mouth. Clearly the swamps round the great river afforded no healthy land for settling. There must be more exploration done, and meantime his wife and children must be cared for. They were hundreds of miles from any white settlement. Even so, Livingstone might still have debated his mission. Nevertheless, revelations came to him that the slaver was even now establishing his accursed hold on this district. Sebituane's people, the Makololo, who were loyal tribesmen, had begun to sell children plundered from their native villages for guns and calicoes. "It is brokenheartedness," he wrote much later, "of which the slaves die. Even children, who showed wonderful endurance in keeping up with the chained gangs, would sometimes hear the sound of dancing and the merry tinkle of drums in passing near a village; then the memory of home and happy days proved too much for them, they cried and sobbed, the broken heart came on, and they rapidly sank." This was the awful revelation that came to Livingstone in the land of the Makololo. Little more than a year before, such an idea as the barter of human beings for guns had never been known among this tribe. "Had we been here sooner the slave traffic would never have existed," argued Livingstone.

He began to have a vision of Christian settlements standing sentinel over the lives and happiness of the natives of the interior. If the slaver could make his way from the coast to the center, so could the missionary. It was the one effective counter stroke in the battle for human liberty. Nevertheless, it meant separation from wife and children. He must return and do this work alone. He could risk no one's life but his own. His decision was taken. He devotes only a single paragraph to the long and arduous journey to Cape Town. It was a matter of fifteen hundred miles, and part of it was through territory where a so-called Kaffir War[2] was being waged, which excited Livingstone's scorn for the waste of blood and treasure. He was an object of suspicion at the Cape. The State authorities suspected his humanitarian sympathies and the Church officials his theological orthodoxy.

He was in debt, and had been waiting for his small salary to arrive for more than a year. He decided to write to the Directors of the London Missionary Society in the most resolute terms. "Con-

---

[2] The eighth Kaffir War (1850–53), to which Livingstone alludes in this passage, was the most drawn-out and costly of all. These wars were a long-running series of Cape Frontier Wars (1779–1879) between the Boers, now called Afrikaners, and the Xhosa people. The term Kaffir, or "Caffre"

sider the multitudes that in the Providence of God have been brought to light in the country of Sebituane; the probability that in our efforts to evangelize we shall put a stop to the slave trade in a large region, and by means of the high way into the north which we have discovered bring unknown nations into the sympathies of the Christian World.... Nothing but a strong conviction that the step will lead to the Glory of Christ would make me

A portrait of Livingstone taken in Cape Town in 1852 while sending his family back to England.

orphanise my children.... Should you not feel yourselves justified in incurring the expense of their support in England, I shall feel called upon to renounce the hope of carrying the Gospel into that country.... But stay, I am not sure; so powerfully convinced am I that it is the will of our Lord that I should go, I will go, no matter who opposes; but from you I expect nothing but encouragement." A happy comment on this letter is found in Livingstone's *Missionary Travels*, in the paragraph recording the farewell to his wife and children. "Having placed my family on board a homeward bound ship, and promised to rejoin them in two years, we parted for, as it subsequently proved, nearly five years. The Directors of the London Missionary Society signified their cordial approval of my project by leaving the matter entirely to my own discretion, and I have much pleasure in acknowledging my obligations to the gentlemen composing that body for always acting in an enlightened spirit, and with as much liberality as their constitution would allow."

Livingstone started back for the interior on the eighth of June, 1852. He was now in his fortieth year.

(as the British spelled it in Livingstone's day), is an Arabic word that means "unbeliever"; it was introduced by Arab traders and is used as a derogatory term referring to black Africans.

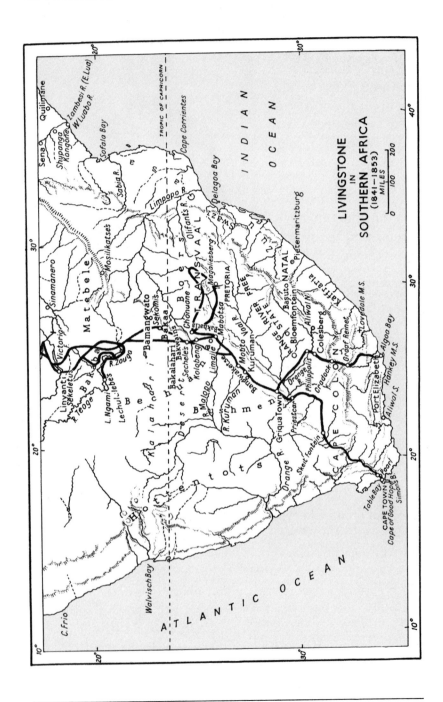

CHAPTER 3

Expedition to Linyanti

1852–1853

It is difficult to summarize Livingstone's achievements during the first eleven years he had spent in Africa. He had penetrated further north from the Cape than any other white man. He had discovered Lake Ngami and the upper reaches of the Zambezi River. He had given Christianity a foothold among the Bakwains and the Makololo. He had been used by God to help convert one of the most remarkable chiefs in Central Africa. He had built three houses with his own hands and had taught many hundreds to read. He had exercised the healing art to the relief and benefit of thousands. He had made some progress in reducing Sechuana to a grammatical language and had even composed hymns in it. He had made invaluable scientific research and had enriched our knowledge of the flora and fauna of Central Africa. Finally, he had seen at first hand the horrors of the slave traffic, and had vowed himself to the ultimate destruction of this form of "man's inhumanity to man." Eleven busy, arduous, and perilous years had brought him to mid-life. He was now about to dedicate all his ripe experience and unique powers of head and heart to the cause of establishing Christ's Kingdom in the hearts of those living in the dark interior of the continent to which he had consecrated his life. Even during his brief sojourn at the Cape he had been perfecting himself for the work that lay before him. He had studied astronomy and had learned to take observations under Sir Thomas Maclear, the Astronomer Royal, who wrote of him afterwards: "What that man has done is unprecedented. You could go to any point across the entire continent along Livingstone's track, and feel certain of your position." In David Livingstone's judgment, it was impossible for a man to be too thoroughly equipped for the great business of a missionary.

In one respect, his equipment was necessarily poor. His financial resources were so meager that he had to fall back on very lean cows to draw his wagon, which is why the journey to Kuruman took a full three months. There a broken wheel detained him, and possibly saved his life; for this was the time selected by the band of Boer marauders to wreak their vengeance on him and on the hapless tribe of Sechéle. It is a shocking story, and in his sympathy with Sechéle, sixty of whose people had been massacred, Livingstone could almost forget his own personal loss, though he grieved sorely over the wanton destruction of his books. Amid all his sorrow and heartbreak, he could still smile at the humorous side. "We shall move more easily now that we are lightened of our furniture. They have taken away our sofa. I never had a good rest on it. We had only got it ready when we left. Well, they can't have taken away all the stones. We shall have a seat in spite of them, and that, too, with a merry heart which doeth good like a medicine." Surely the wise Creator God knew what He was doing as He gave His servant David Livingstone strength to deal with tragedy. He could jest that "the Boers had saved me the trouble of making a will."

Poor Sechéle in his despair resolved on a personal appeal for justice to the great "White Queen" and actually traveled to the Cape to take ship to England. Although he was unable to make such a journey, Sechéle was shown much kindness in the Cape and eventually returned, gathered the people around him, and became a stronger chief than before, while he continued to instruct his tribe in the Bible without any assistance from a missionary. There are few more striking proofs of the enduring power of Livingstone's personal influence and Christian faith.

The journey through the desert to the Chobe River and across it to where Sekelétu, the son of Sebituane, was now reigning, was more arduous and perilous than it had been previously. The floods from the annual inundation of the Chobe were an almost invincible obstacle; yet where the waters did not lie the heat was torrid. "At the surface of the ground in the sun the thermometer registered 125 °F. The hand cannot be held on the earth, and even the callused feet of the natives must be protected by sandals of hide."

The battle with the waters of the Chobe and its tributaries would have ended in the defeat of anyone less lionhearted than this stubborn Scottish missionary. Many of the natives retired from the encounter on the weak pretext of throwing dice and declaring that the "gods" willed their return. Some of them feigned sickness to ride in the wagons, and it required infinite patience and humoring to get them forward. Part of the journey lay through dense forest, and laborious days were spent swinging the ax to make a wagon track. The rivers effectually stopped the wagons; and Livingstone took to a pontoon, and afterwards to canoes. Nevertheless, there was much wading to do under a blistering sun, and through reeds that "made our hands all raw and bloody," and thorns that tore even leather trousers. They were glad to sleep in a filthy deserted hut, and at night the cold dews descended and the mosquitoes gathered in clouds. They were disturbed by the hippopotami, and the eerie waters were alive with water snakes. No combination of perils, however, had any terror for one whose creed was that "man is immortal till his work on earth is done." At twilight one day, a village was spotted on the river bank. It was Morémi, and Livingstone had reached his beloved Makololo at last. "The inhabitants looked like people who had seen a ghost," he says, but what he himself really looked like he forbears to add. "He has dropped among us from the clouds, yet came riding on the back of a hippopotamus,"—this was their appropriate description of the pontoon. "We Makololo thought no one could cross the Chobe without our knowledge, but here he drops among us like a bird." They returned with him, "took the wagons to pieces and carried them across on a number of canoes lashed together." On the twenty-third of May 1853, they reached Linyanti, the capital town of the Makololo, where the new chief, Sekelétu, received them "in royal style."

The tired missionary was hopeful that this location would suit his needs. Livingstone was initially encouraged to note that Sekelétu was not a whit behind Sebituane in friendliness and not much inferior in intelligence. He had no desire for the Bible, fearing that it might compel him to content himself with one wife.

He set an example to the tribe, however, in reverent attention to Livingstone's simple preaching, and he had absolute faith in the protection afforded to his people by Livingstone's presence and skill. Exactly a week after the arrival at Linyanti, however, Livingstone had his first taste of malaria, and the well-meant efforts of the native doctors did not do much to cure him. He experienced its weakening effect. If he looked up suddenly, he was affected with a strange giddiness. "Everything appeared to rush to the left, and if I did not catch hold of some support I fell heavily on the ground." The same horrible sensations occurred at night, "whenever I turned suddenly round." One thing was clear— Linyanti was no place for a healthy settlement. Some might add that with fever in the system it was foolish to think of a journey of a thousand miles or more. Nevertheless, this was not Livingstone's way of looking at things. "There is a good deal in not giving in to this disease," he writes; "he who is low-spirited will die sooner than the man who is not of a melancholic nature."

Sick as he was, he was resolute to continue his explorations, and with Sekelétu and a large band of Makololo for companions, he traveled some hundreds of miles of waterway, ascending the great river to the northwest from Seshéke. Here the Zambezi is called the Leeambye, and Livingstone expressed his delight at skimming along in great canoes, gazing on a wonderful inland river which no white man had hitherto explored. He found, as ever, in the wonders and beauties of nature, the splendor of the wild birds, and the curious fascination of the river beasts some relief from the awful spectacle, constantly present, of human cruelty and degradation. "The sciences," he writes, "exhibit such wonderful intelligence and design in all their various ramifications, some time ought to be devoted to them before engaging in missionary work.... We may feel that we are leaning on His bosom while living in a world clothed in beauty, and robed with the glorious perfection of its Maker and Preserver.... He who stays his mind on his ever-present, ever-energetic God, will not fret himself because of evildoers. He that believeth shall not make haste."

It was indeed well for him that he had been given the grace to absorb himself in "whatsoever things are lovely," for the nightmare of heathenism was always with him. He had to witness Sekelétu's revenge on those who had plotted against him. Some of the scenes were incredibly horrible, and his protests were unavailing. The miseries of slavery wrung his heart, and as he advanced into the dark interior, the chorus of human agonies was ever in his ears. "I was in closer contact with heathens than I had ever been before, and though all were as kind to me as possible, yet to endure the dancing, roaring and singing, the jesting, the grumbling, quarreling and murdering of these children of nature was the severest penance I had yet undergone in the course of my missionary duties."

Again he exclaimed in his diary, "the more intimately I become acquainted with barbarians, the more disgusting does heathenism become. It is inconceivably vile.... They never visit anywhere but for the purpose of plunder and oppression. They never go anywhere but with a club or spear in hand.... They need a healer. May God enable me to be such to them." Slowly but surely the whole tragedy of Africa was unveiled before him. The fair landscape of its rivers and forests, the gay plumage of its birds, and beauty of its living creatures, was like a gorgeous curtain covering unspeakable depths of pain and sin. The people gathered in hundreds to hear him, and especially to see the wonders of his magic lantern (a primitive form of a slide projector), but he could not in a brief stay undo the superstitions and inhumanities of centuries. His eye was on the future. "A minister who has not seen so much pioneer service as I have done would have been shocked to see so little effect produced by an earnest discourse concerning judgment, but time must be given to allow the truth to sink into the dark mind and produce its effect. The earth shall be filled with the knowledge of the glory of the Lord—that is enough. We can afford to work in faith, for Omnipotence is pledged to fulfill the promise...."

Baffled in the hope of finding a healthy situation for a permanent mission station near Linyanti, the final determination to make a way to the coast crystallized in his mind. "I shall open up a path to the interior or perish," he writes in his terse, decisive way to Dr. Moffat; "I never have had the shadow of a shade of doubt as to the propriety of my course." On November 8, he wrote home to his father what he evidently felt may be his last will and testament: "May God in mercy permit me to do something for the cause of Christ in these dark places of the earth. May He accept my children for His service and sanctify them for it. My blessing on my wife. May God comfort her! If my watch comes back after I am cut off, it belongs to Agnes. If my sextant, it is Robert's. The Paris medal to Thomas. Double-barreled gun to Zouga. Be a father to the fatherless and a husband to the widow for Jesus' sake." That was all. Some Boers had relieved him of the necessity of willing any other belongings. He had none.

CHAPTER 4

March to Luanda

1853–1854

Before we begin our journey with Livingstone to the coast, it will be well to pause and consider two things—firstly, the task proposed; and secondly, the equipment for the task.

(1)   **The Task.** Linyanti lies a hundred miles from the Zambezi River, at which the two possible routes may be said to fork. The one, eastward, was comparatively simple: it was to follow the great river some thousand miles to the sea. The other, westward, meant tracing the river towards the source so far as was possible, and then striking westward for St. Paul de Loanda (modern day Luanda), a matter in all of some fifteen hundred miles. Cape Town lay to the south, another fifteen hundred miles. These were the three spokes of the wheel from the center at Linyanti. Little was known to Livingstone of either the eastward or the westward route. He could only roughly estimate the distance. He had no notion what hostile tribes, what malarial swamps, what impenetrable forests, what waterless deserts might be encountered. All that lay in the hands of Providence. He had not only to make this pilgrimage himself; he had to watch over the safety of his Makololo men, keep them supplied with food and drink, and protect them in the event of attack by savages. The deadly tsetse fly[3] lay in wait for his oxen. The African fever lurked in ambush everywhere. Perils of floods and fevers, wild beasts and wilder human foes might be expected as a daily portion. Death

---

[3] A bloodsucking fly of Africa, which can carry and transmit sleeping sickness and other illnesses.

would be almost a familiar companion. No love of adventure, no curiosity and fascination of exploration would have driven Livingstone through this self-imposed task. One has only to study his journal and listen to his simple, artless confessions of faith to see that at every step the Christian motive was supreme. He had sight of the ultimate City—the coming civilization of Christ—and the lions on the way were all chained, and the dangerous rapids subdued.

(2) **The Equipment for the Task.** Seldom was a journey of such heroic proportions undertaken with such simple equipment. When one reads of the elaborate preparations for modern expeditions not half so formidable, one is amazed at the contrast. Some of my readers may have heard of the four tin canisters, fifteen inches square, that held all of Livingstone's valuables. One contained spare shirts, trousers, and shoes to be used when civilization was reached. One was a medicine chest. One a library. One held the "magic" lantern by means of which the Gospel story was to be preached. For the rest, there were twenty pounds of beads, value forty shillings, a few biscuits, a few pounds of tea and sugar, and about twenty pounds of coffee. There were five guns in all: three muskets for the natives who could use them and who only hit things by accident; a rifle and double-barreled shotgun for Livingstone, whose injured arm always made shooting difficult, and whose fever-shaken frame sometimes made it impossible. A bag of clothes for the journey, a small tent, a sheepskin mantle, and a horse-rug to sleep on completed this equipment. The sextant and other instruments were carried separately; and the ammunition was "distributed through the luggage," so that if any portion were lost some powder and shot would remain for them. Twenty-seven men were chosen for

the westward journey; and it is as well to set down the fact here that all the twenty-seven were brought back in safety to their homes.

The expedition left Linyanti on the eleventh of November 1853. Away in Europe, the English and French fleets had entered the Bosphorus, and a delirious public opinion was hurrying Great Britain into the blunders of the Crimean War. Far away from all the "fool-furies" of European politics, one single-minded Christian hero was setting his heart on the more renowned victories of peace and freedom, with nothing to sustain him but his own quenchless faith in God and a noble task. Even at the start he had been severely shaken with fever, and much preaching had brought back an old troublesome complaint in the throat; but these were personal inconveniences which he never allowed to deter him from any line of duty. The farewells were said with Sekelétu at Seshéke on the Zambezi, and the expedition passed away to the northwest into the great unknown.

For the particulars of Livingstone's memorable journeys we are dependent on what he called his "lined journal." It was a strongly bound quarto[4] volume of more than eight hundred pages, and fitted with lock and key. The writing in it is extraordinarily neat and clear; but there are pathetic pages in which the writer is evidently shaking with fever—yet nevertheless his iron will is compelling his trembling fingers to do their duty. Everything went down in his journal. Dr. Blaikie well says that "it is built up in a random-rubble style." There are frequent prayers and poignant religious reflections, the expressions of a heart charged to overflowing with the Divine love and human compassion. Immediately following will be scientific observations, or speculations on some problem of natural history or geological structure. The various incidents in the journey are all recorded with the simplicity and freedom from sensationalism of the Evangelist Mark. Livingstone never magnifies a peril and dwells not at all on his personal heroism. The "lined journal" ranks as one of his "books," and its companions in the little canister were

---

[4] A book about the size 9.5 inches by 12 inches formed by folding whole sheets of paper (19 inches by 24 inches) into four leaves, or eight pages.

only a Sechuana Pentateuch, Thomson's Tables, a Nautical Almanac, and a Bible. He confesses that "the want of other mental pabulum is felt severely."

A setback little short of a disaster befell him at the beginning of this journey. The greater part of his medicines were stolen. With the health of all his escort weighing upon him and with fever racking his own frame, it must have seemed as if the potential of success was obviously diminished. It is interesting to compare Livingstone's rate of progress with that of ordinary traders. The trader thought seven miles a day good traveling, and even so he only reckoned on traveling ten days a month. Seventy miles a month was, in his eye, satisfactory progress. Livingstone struck an average of ten miles a day, and traveled about twenty days a month. Thus he seldom made less than two hundred miles a month. He traveled from Linyanti to Luanda (some 1,400 miles) in six months and a half, which as a mere feat of rapid African transit was quite amazing. On this journey he rode hundreds of miles on the back of his riding-ox, Sindbad, whose temper was uncertain and whose idiosyncrasies were pronounced. We shall see as we proceed that Sindbad was by no means always a satisfactory colleague.

Complications that might have led to ugly developments occurred while they were still in Sekelétu's sphere of influence and among his people. It was discovered that a party of Makololo had made a foray to the north and had destroyed some of the villages of the Balonda, through whose country they were bound to pass. Some of the villagers had been seized for slaves, and Livingstone foresaw reprisals and the probability that prejudice would be excited against himself and his men. He therefore insisted that the captives should be restored, as a means of demonstrating that his errand was one of friendliness and peace. This act helped to disarm the hostility of the Balonda chief, and Livingstone afterwards busied himself to form a commercial alliance between the Balonda and the Makololo. It was always his policy to overcome the jealousies and hostilities of rival tribes and substitute confidence based on mutual interest.

After leaving the country of the Makololo, and while ascending the Barotse Valley, the rains were almost incessant, and the

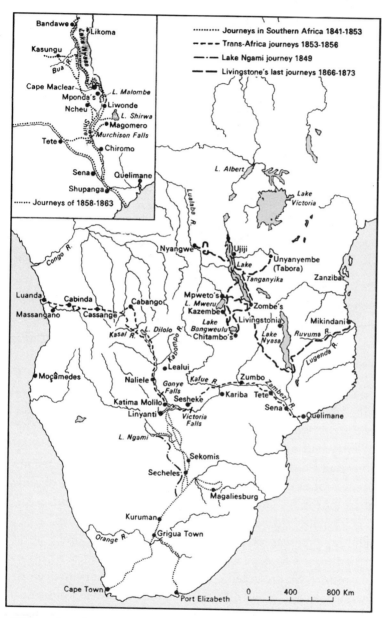

This map shows the various journeys made by David Livingstone throughout Southern Africa. Note the distance of the Trans-Africa journeys in particular.

expedition moved forward through clouds of vapor that hardly ever lifted. For a whole fortnight, neither sun nor moon was seen sufficiently to get an observation for latitude and longitude. The very tent that sheltered him by night began to rot with the excessive and incessant humidity. In spite of being kept well oiled, the guns grew rusty; and the clothing of the party became "moldy and rotten." Part of the way lay through dense forest, and the ax had continually to be plied. The waters of the river were crowded with hippopotami, crocodiles, and at times with fish; but it was not easy to get food in the forest, and repeatedly they were reduced to living on such roots as could be trusted, while moles and mice became a luxury. They were heading now for the country of the great chief Shinté, whose fame had traveled far; and early in the new year of 1854 found them at his capital, the most imposing town that Livingstone had seen in Central Africa. In the town were two Portuguese traders who were dealing for slaves and ivory. "They had a gang of young female slaves in a chain, hoeing the ground in front of their encampment." This was the first time that Livingstone's Barotse companions had seen slaves in chains. "They are not men," they exclaimed (meaning they are beasts), "who treat their children so."

> It seemed to Livingstone that, as they moved north, the moral conditions darkened. At times the great horror of heathenism laid hold of him. Everywhere was the same unrelieved tragedy of brutality and murder.

The explorer was received with great ceremony. Shinté sat on a "sort of throne" covered with a leopard's skin, under a banyan tree. He must have presented a somewhat bizarre appearance, for Livingstone tells us "he had on a checked jacket and a kilt of scarlet, baize-edged with green." Strings of beads, copper armlets, and bracelets hung about his neck and limbs. For a crown he had a great helmet made of beads and surmounted with a huge bunch of goose feathers. The subsequent ceremony was as odd and elaborate as the chief's wardrobe. There were terrifying maneuvers of savage soldiers armed to the teeth. Livingstone suspected that their object was to cause him and his friends to take to their heels, but if so it was a failure. At last, the newcomers were presented to the chief by the orator Sambanza, who described Livingstone's exploits in great style, dwelling on the fact that he had brought back the captives taken by the Makololo, that he possessed "the Word from Heaven," that he sought the peace of all the tribes, and was opening up a path for trade.

This speech was a great effort, and its effect was by no means minimized by the fact that the orator wore "a cloth so long that a boy carried it after him as a train." It would appear that fashionable habits are the same all the world over. During his stay at Shinté's court, Livingstone suffered agonies from fever, accompanied by "violent action of the heart." Nevertheless, he made his own invariable impression upon the chief by his frankness, independence, and courtesy. He preached to the assembled tribesmen and showed the magic-lantern pictures; he pleaded urgently with Shinté personally against the growing practice of slavery. When his stay was over, Shinté gave him the last evidence of good will, for "he drew from out of his clothing a string of beads and the end of a conical shell, which is considered in regions far from the sea of as great value as the Lord Mayor's badge is in London. He hung it round my neck, and said, 'There now you *have* a proof of my friendship.'" Shinté also bequeathed to the expedition his "principal guide" Mtemése, who he promised would conduct them to the sea.

Mtemése proved to be by no means an immaculate person. Among other delinquencies, he left the pontoon behind, a loss that was keenly felt. He also had a prejudice against speedy travel which Livingstone could not be induced to share. He was useful, however, in levying tribute of food throughout Shinté's dominion, and evidently thought Livingstone a great fool for paying a fair price for what could have been had for nothing. Gradually Shinté's territory was left behind, and that of Katema was invaded. It seemed to Livingstone that, as they moved north, the moral conditions darkened. At times the great horror of heathenism laid hold of him. Everywhere was the same unrelieved tragedy of brutality and murder. Sometimes over the camp fires his savage hosts would brag about their customs. They told of the death of chiefs and the slaughter of enough of their subjects to fill any mind with horror. The further north Livingstone penetrated the more "superstitious" did the people become. Yet he must eat with them, chat with them, laugh with them; and the impression of such religious teaching as he could impart was, alas! so superficial. Katema proved peaceable; but his people lived under the perpetual shadow of the slave trade and would gladly have been taken away to the Makololo country.

The beginning of March found them for the first time in hostile territory. There had been much rain and flood, wading and swimming. Livingstone himself had had an adventure that thoroughly alarmed his men, and served to evoke their real devotion. He was flung from his ox in midstream, and compelled to strike out for the opposite bank. There was a simultaneous rush on the part of all his men to rescue him. Their delight was unbounded when they found he could swim like themselves. "Who carried the white man across the river but himself," they said afterwards.

It was among the Chiboques that the expedition came nearest to having to fight for their lives; and bloodshed was only averted by Livingstone's wonderful patience and fearlessness. He sat on a camp stool with his double-barreled gun across his knees and insisted on arguing with the chief who was endeavoring to levy blackmail. It was characteristic of Livingstone that he argued the legitimacy of passing through their country on the ground that the land belonged to God. If their gardens had been damaged compensation would have been paid, but the earth is the Lord's. "They did not attempt to controvert this," he comments, "because it is in accordance with their own ideas." Finally he told them that if there was to be a fight they must begin it, and the guilt be on their heads. Matters looked critical for some hours; but Livingstone's tact prevailed, and the gift of an ox satisfied them for the time being.

They had more trouble later before they could get beyond the land of the Chiboques, but there was no actual outbreak. There was thieving of their goods, however, which were getting sadly reduced, and the attitude of enmity and treachery added to the gloom of a very gloomy forest through which a way had to be found. So thick was the atmosphere that the hanging creepers could not be seen, and again and again the riders were swept off the backs of the oxen. On one occasion Sindbad went off at a plunging gallop, the bridle broke, and Livingstone

It was a weak, worn, haggard figure that on the thirty-first of May 1854, entered the city of Luanda, "laboring under great depression of spirits...." Nevertheless, he had finished his course.... He had reached the coast. He had protected and guided his faithful company. He had robbed no man's goods and taken no man's life, and all the fourteen hundred miles he had preached the Gospel and argued for freedom and peace.

came down backwards on the crown of his head. At the same time, Sindbad completed the triumph by dealing him a kick on the thigh. Livingstone makes light of all this, only remarking that "he does not recommend it as a remedy for fever." Repeated attacks of fever had reduced him to a skeleton. The sodden blanket which served as a saddle caused abrasions and sores. His "projecting bones" were chafed on the hard bed at nights. He had enough burdens to bear without having to dare the threats of savages. At the last outpost of the Chiboque country, their two guides turned traitors and thieves and escaped with the larger portion of their beads, so necessary for barter. This was almost the last straw; there was mutiny among Livingstone's men, for they declared they would go home. He was in despair; having finally told them that in that case he would go on alone, he went into his little tent and flung himself upon his knees, "with the mind directed to Him who hears the sighing of the soul." Presently, one of the men crept into the tent. "We will never leave you," he said. "Do not be disheartened. Wherever you lead, we will follow." The others took up the chorus. They were all his children, they told him, and they would die for him. They had only spoken in the bitterness of their feeling and felt they could do nothing.

They had one more parley with a bullying chief, but came out victorious, thanks to the opportune appearance of a young Portuguese military officer, who afterwards showed them every hospitality. Moreover, they were now able to dispose of certain tusks of ivory presented to them by Sekelétu, the proceeds of which clothed the whole party and partially armed them. The journey was easy now, save that the intrepid leader had had twenty-seven attacks of fever, and suffered one more humiliation at the hands of Sindbad, being compelled inadvertently to bathe in the Lombé. He had to reassure his men as they drew near to the Atlantic, for they began to be troubled lest after all he should leave them to the cruel mercies of other white men. "Nothing will happen to you but what happens to me," he told them. "We have stood by one another hitherto and will do so till the last." In course of time, they crossed the sterile plains near Luanda, and gazed upon the sea. "We marched along with our father," they said afterwards, "believing that what the ancients had always told us was true, that the world has no end; but all at once the world said to us, 'I am finished, there is no more of me.'"

It was a weak, worn, haggard figure that on the thirty-first of May 1854, entered the city of Luanda, "laboring under great depression of spirits." The fever had brought on chronic dysentery. He could not sit on his ox ten minutes at a time. His mind was "depressed by disease and care." His heart misgave him as to his welcome. Nevertheless, he had finished his course. He had accomplished his superhuman task. He had reached the coast. He had protected and guided his faithful company. He had robbed no man's goods and taken no man's life, and all the fourteen hundred miles he had preached the Gospel and argued for freedom and peace.

CHAPTER 5

Man of Honor

1854–1856

Livingstone found Luanda a very decayed town, but he did not fail to win many friendships. Mr. Gabriel, the one Englishman in the place, was overwhelmingly kind, and the Roman Catholic bishop scarcely less so. English men-of-war were in the harbor also, keeping both eyes open for slave ships, and Livingstone was able to take his men on board and show them the cannon with which England "was going to destroy the slave trade."

He himself recovered only very slowly from his condition of absolute emaciation and in August had a severe relapse, which left him a mere skeleton. Everybody was kind to him, encouraging him and nourishing him, and, what was of greatest benefit in his depression, providing him with lively and interesting company. He fell in with their plans for him very gratefully, but on one point he was adamant. They had wished to persuade him to go home and rest. The British captains offered him a passage to St. Helena. When this failed, they urged him to take the mail-packet, the *Forerunner*, by which all his own precious diaries, letters, and scientific papers, with maps and so forth, were to be sent. Despite his weakness it was not in him to be idle, and he had laboriously accomplished the writing of this big budget of dispatches in time for the mail-boat. On April 23, 1852, he had told his wife that he would rejoin her in two years. It was now August 1854, and his heart cried out for wife and children. Nevertheless, one thing stood in the way. He had promised his twenty-seven men to take them back to their own country; and they were there in Luanda on the faith of Livingstone's word. It did not square with his sense of honor to leave them at Luanda while he went home for a holiday, and he refused all the tempting offers. The reward of honorable men does not always come as it came to him.

The *Forerunner* went down a few days later with all hands but one, and Livingstone escaped an almost certain death because he kept his promise. Alas! All his precious papers, the fruit of so much labor, were destroyed, and he had to take up the drudgery of doing everything over again. It was the form of toil most irksome to him, but he just dug in and did it. It was his way.

By God's grace he had not gone far on the homeward track when this news reached him, and there was no lack of hospitality. He was making a circuit round about Luanda to visit some of the more noted Portuguese settlements and estates, always with an eye to the better cultivation of the country and the interest of inland trade. The rewriting of his papers involved long and tedious delay, and there was more trouble with fever among his men. The year 1855 dawned before he left a hospitable Portuguese home and struck out along the old trail. It is worthwhile to remember here that whereas the expedition traveled from Linyanti to Luanda in six and a half months, it took twice that time to return. It was September 1855, before they saw Linyanti again.

The homeward journey was not devoid of incident and excitement. The passage through the Chiboque territory was once again troublesome. Just when Livingstone was most anxious to be his energetic self, he fell victim to rheumatic fever. For eight days he lay in his tent, tossing and groaning with pain; it was twenty days before he began to recover, and the old ambition to be on the march came back to him. His men objected, for he was too weak to move, and at the physical crisis a quarrel broke out between his men and some of the Chiboques. A blow was struck, for which ample compensation was paid; but with the leader on his back, the importunities of the tribesmen increased and matters became threatening. When a forward move was made, an organized attack on the baggage took place, and shots were even fired, though nobody was hurt. It was then that Livingstone snatched up his six-cylinder revolver and "staggered along the path" till most opportunely he encountered the hostile chief. "The sight of the revolver gaping into his stomach and my own ghastly visage looking daggers at his face seemed to produce an instant revolution in his martial feelings." He suddenly became the most peaceable man in all Africa, and protested his good will. Livingstone advised a practical illustration of this, and bade him go home. The Chief explained that he would do so, only he was afraid of being shot in the back! "If I wanted to kill you," rejoined Livingstone, "I could shoot you in the face as well." One of his men, afraid for Livingstone's own safety, advised him not to give the Chief an occasion to shoot him in the back, whereupon Livingstone retorted, "Tell him to observe that I am not afraid of him," and mounting his ox, rode away triumphantly.

Plodding steadily onward, they arrived on the eighth of June at a spot famous for one of Livingstone's most notable geographical discoveries, which he afterwards learned was actual confirmation of Sir Roderick Murchison's theory, which the latter had worked out in his own armchair as the only one that would satisfy what was known of the African river systems and the geological formation. Livingstone had just forded a wide river called the Lotembwa, only three feet deep, and had failed to remark in which direction it was flowing. He believed it to be the same river that flowed south from Lake Dilolo, but a chief pointed out to him that this was not so, for the former river flowed north into the Kasai, one of the main tributaries of the Congo. The latter flowed south into the Zambezi. Livingstone now realized that he was "standing on the central ridge that divided these two systems," and what amazed him most was the fact that these vast river systems had their rise not in a chain of lofty mountains but on flat plains not more than four thousand feet above the sea.

The expedition now made slow and peaceful progress along their former route, being welcomed everywhere by their old friends with demonstrations of joy and astonishment. They distributed presents to all who had prospered them on their way, and left none but friendly memories behind them. When at the end of July they reached Libonta their progress became a triumphal procession. His men arrayed themselves in white European clothing, swaggered like soldiers, and called themselves his "braves." During the time of service, they sat with their guns over their shoulders. "You have opened a path for us," said the people, "and we shall have sleep." The ovations continued all down the Barotse Valley. There were no drawbacks, except that many of the men found that during their absence some of their wives had sought and found other husbands. Livingstone advised them to console themselves with those that remained. "Even so, you have as many as I have," he reminded them. At Linyanti, Livingstone found his wagon and belongings perfectly safe, some supplies, and a letter a year old from Dr. and Mrs. Moffat. Sekelétu's gratification knew no bounds. A grand new uniform had been sent him as a present from the coast,

> "No one ever gains much influence in this country without purity and uprightness. The acts of a stranger are keenly scrutinized by both old and young...." This illustrates Livingstone's favorite doctrine, that it is the missionary's life that is the most powerful sermon.

and when he wore it to church on Sunday it produced a greater impression than the sermon. It is worth remarking that Sekelétu at once began a trade in ivory with the Portuguese at the coast, in fulfillment of Livingstone's policy.

For eight weeks Livingstone remained at Linyanti. He found plenty to occupy him. He was once again the guide, philosopher, and friend to all the tribe. He had doctoring to do and operations to perform. He found personal interviews on religious subjects more satisfactory than the public services, and he was now, as ever, supremely anxious that these people should embrace the Gospel of Jesus Christ. He had letters to write, journals to transcribe, and new observations to make. He had all the odd jobs to do that had accumulated during his absence. He found Sekelétu a willing pupil in his ideas on commerce and on the removal of the tribe to the healthier and wealthier Barotse Valley. Especially he had to think out the problem of his next great adventure to the East Coast. His inclination decidedly was to trace the course of the Zambezi River to

Quilimane, in Portuguese East Africa (now called Mozambique), and the sea. Nevertheless, this area had an evil reputation for the savagery of some of the tribes along the banks. Certain Arabs whom he had met had strongly counseled him to strike up country to the northeast and make for Zanzibar by the south of Lake Tanganyika. The tribes were reported to be peaceable and the villages and food supplies plentiful. If he decided to explore the Zambezi, the problem of the north or south shore was an important one. The north shore was reported to be very rocky and broken, and consequently especially difficult for transport.

Either shore was likely to be dangerous to the oxen on account of the tsetse fly. All these considerations had to be weighed, but the final decision was to risk the dangers of the tribes along the Zambezi and to take the north shore because on Livingstone's map, Tete, the farthest inland station of the Portuguese, was marked as being on the north of the river. This turned out to be untrue. Having settled his course, he made his preparations. Sekelétu proved himself a most magnificent ally. Livingstone's new escort was composed of a hundred and twenty men, with ten slaughter oxen and three of the best riding oxen. He was provided with stores of food, and given tribute rights over all tribes subject to Sekelétu. When we consider that Livingstone had no one to finance him and that the success of his travels depended on the good will of native chiefs like Sekelétu, we begin to understand the unique influence which he exercised over the native mind. Those who knew him never failed him when in a pinch; they never deserted him in his need; they lent their best aid to carry through his enterprises and gave him every tangible proof that can be given from one man to another of confidence, honor, and love.

Perhaps before we set out on this new journey we may quote from Livingstone himself two passages illustrative of the secret of his influence. In the first he says, "No one ever gains much influence in this country without purity and uprightness. The acts of a stranger are keenly scrutinized by both old and young, and seldom is the judgment pronounced even by a heathen unfair or uncharitable. I have heard women speaking in admiration of a white man because he was pure, and never was guilty of any secret immorality. Had he been, they would have known it, and, untutored heathen though they be, would have despised him in consequence." This illustrates Livingstone's favorite doctrine, that it is the missionary's life that is the most powerful sermon. That his teaching was partially understood may be gathered from the story of Mamire, Sekelétu's stepfather, who on coming to say good-bye, used words like these: "You are now going among people who cannot be trusted because we have used them badly, but you go with a different message from any they ever heard before, and Jesus will be with you, and help you, though among enemies." It was a gracious and discerning Godspeed.

The route selected led Livingstone across what we know today as Zimbabwe, and which would have been much more appropriately named Livingstonia. It passed to the north of the land inhabited by the formidable and dreaded Matabele. The tribes bordering on the Makololo country had no reason to love their oppressive neighbors, and this fact had inspired the fears expressed in Mamire's words. It was on the third of November 1855, that the final departure from Linyanti was made, and Sekelétu accompanied the expedition along the first stage. He took the opportunity of showing Livingstone an extraordinary kindness, for the journey began in a terrific tropical thunderstorm. Livingstone's clothing had gone on, and there was nothing to do but to sleep on the cold ground. Sekelétu, however, took his own blanket and wrapped it about the missionary, lying himself uncovered through the cold night. "I was much affected," writes Livingstone, "by this little act of genuine kindness. If such men must perish by the advance of civilization, as certain races of animals do before others, it is a pity."

It was no great distance to the famous falls, the rumor of which had often reached Livingstone, and which he was the first white man to visit. The falls were originally called Shongwe. Sebituane used to ask Livingstone whether in his own country he had "smoke that thunders," referring to the pillars of vapor and the far-carrying roar of the river as it plunged into the chasm beneath. Sliding down the river in their canoes, they came to within half a mile of the falls, when some of the natives who were expert in the management of the rapids transferred Livingstone to a lighter canoe, and with practiced dexterity guided it to the central island—the "Goat (Livingstone) Is-

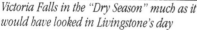

Victoria Falls in the "Dry Season" much as it would have looked in Livingstone's day

land" of the Zambezi falls—"on the edge of the lip over which the water rolls." This adventure can only be made when the river is low, but it was successfully accomplished, and Livingstone was able to gaze down into the fissure into which the great river plunges and apparently disappears. Then he saw that "a stream of a thousand yards [actually 1,800 yards] broad leaped down a hundred feet [actually 350 feet], and then became suddenly compressed into a space of fifteen or twenty yards." He spent many hours contemplating its beauties, noting all its fascinations, and pondering the scientific problem of its origin. He then permitted himself the only act of nationalism—"personal vanity" he used to call it—that he ever indulged in. He changed the native name to Victoria Falls in honor of the great "White Queen." Returning to the island the next day with Sekelétu, he carved his initials and the date on a tree and planted "about a hundred peach and apricot stones and a quantity of coffee seeds," with the observation that, if

This statue of Livingstone, stands on the Zimbabwe side of Victoria Falls, next to "Devil's Cataract." The inscriptions on the plaques commemorate the life and work of the pioneer missionary/explorer as the first white man to see the falls.

there were no hippopotami, he had no doubt this would become the parent of all the gardens which may yet be planted in this newly discovered land.

Sekelétu now returned home, having provided a company of 114 men to carry the tusks to the coast, and the expedition set forth in a northward direction. Many wars had decimated the country, but there were ample evidences of the savagery of the people, as well. He found one old chief living in a house surrounded with human skulls, much like Giant Pope's cave in the *Pilgrim's Progress*. Many of the skulls were of mere children, slain by the chief's father "to show his fierceness." The Batoka tribe could be recognized because of their custom of knocking out the upper front teeth at the age of puberty, which gave them an uncouth appearance and a hideous laugh. He found them "very degraded" and much addicted to smoking the *mutokwana*, a pernicious weed which causes a kind of frenzy, and which is often resorted to before battle as the native form of "Dutch courage"—courage inspired by liquor.

On the fourth of December, they had a foretaste of coming peril in the person of a howling maniac, who came at Livingstone with his lips covered with foam and with a small battle-ax in his hand. "I felt it would be a sorry way to leave the world, to get my head chopped by a mad man" but he would show no fear, and by and by the paroxysm of frenzy passed away. Later on, they heard the tribesmen exulting over them. "God has apportioned them to us," they cried. Still there was no outbreak, and the expedition moved on unmolested. The country was now seen to be swarming with inhabitants. They had no notion of any invasion of their territory that did not mean conquest and plunder, but when the villagers listened to Christ's promise of "Peace on earth, good will to men," they expressed satisfaction. "Give us rest and sleep," they pleaded. Further on, the chief Monze was urgent that a white man should come and live among his people, and his sister seconded him, exclaiming that it would be joy "to sleep without dreaming of anyone pursuing one with a spear."

They traveled on through a healthy and beautiful region where Livingstone could indulge to the full his love of natural beauties and study the habits of the wonderful beasts and birds. They kept well to the north of the Zambezi, and the first organized hostility awaited them at the joining of the Zambezi and the Loangwa. There is no more striking or characteristic story than this in the whole of Livingstone's biography. The chief Mburuma had shown many signs of treachery and had stirred up the countryside against the expedition. It seemed almost certain that the passage of the Loangwa would be contested. The people were gathering in large numbers and remained in obstinate suspicion at a distance from the camp. Livingstone's own reflections are to be gathered from the entries in his journal. On January fourteenth—for 1856 has come—he writes,

"Thank God for His great mercies this far. How soon I may be called before Him, my righteous Judge, I know not…. On Thy word I lean. The cause is Thine. See, O Lord, how the heathens rise up against me as they did against Thy Son." Then comes a very characteristic sentence: "It seems a pity that the facts about the two healthy longitudinal regions should not be known in Christendom. Thy will be done."

Later on in the evening, the signs are even more ominous. "Felt much turmoil of spirit in view of having all my plans for the welfare of this great region and teeming population knocked on the head by savages tomorrow. But Jesus came and said, 'All power is given to Me in Heaven and on earth. Go ye therefore and teach all nations… and lo! I am with you always, even unto the end of the world.' It is the word of a Gentleman of the most sacred and strictest honor and there is no discharge in God's army. I will not cross furtively [i.e., secretly] by night as I intended. It would appear as flight, and should such a man as I flee? Nay, verily, I shall take observations for longitude and latitude tonight, though they may be the last. I feel quite calm now, thank God." The next day he superintended the crossing of the river, under the cover of natives armed to the teeth, reserving for himself the post of honor, the last man in the last canoe. He stepped in, pushed off, thanked the astonished savages, and wished them peace. Then "passing through the midst of them, he went his way." They had never seen an enemy like this.

New perils arose in the country of the powerful chief Mpende, and again Livingstone had little hope of avoiding a skirmish. Nevertheless, he succeeded in explaining that he was an Englishman, and showed them his white skin. "No," said they, "we never saw skin so white as that. You must be one of the tribe that loves the black men." He accepted the compliment, and when later he needed a canoe to take a sick man across the river, Mpende exclaimed, "this white man is truly one of our friends. See how he lets me know his afflictions."

He was now on the south side of the river, and the natives were peaceful. The second of March saw the expedition within eight miles of Tete, and Portuguese officers came forward to help and welcome him. He succeeded in making arrangements for his Makololo to be cared for until his return, for he could now descend the river by boat to Quilimane. Nothing but death, he told them, would prevent his return. He resolved to take Sekwelou, the leader of his escort, to England with him. The result was tragic. The extraordinary experience of a sea voyage unhinged his reason, and when Mauritius was reached, Sekwelou sprang overboard and was lost.

On December 12, 1856, David Livingstone reached Dover, having narrowly escaped shipwreck off the Bay of Tunis, and having crossed the Continent from Marseilles to Calais. He had girdled Africa from West to East. He was universally recognized as the greatest of explorers. Well might Dr. Moffat write to him, "the honors awaiting you at home would be enough to make a score of light heads dizzy.... You have succeeded beyond the most sanguine [i.e., bloodstained] expectation in laying open a world of [seemingly] immortal beings, all needing the Gospel, and at a time, now that war is over, when people may exert their energies on an object compared with that which has occupied the master minds of Europe, expended so much money, and shed so much blood, is but a phantom." Livingstone's own simple words are the best conclusion to this chapter: "None has cause for more abundant gratitude to his fellowmen and to his Maker than I have; and may God grant that the effect on my mind be such that I may be more humbly devoted to the service of the Author of all our mercies."

The veteran missionary to Africa finally arrived home for a much needed rest.

CHAPTER 6

The Tragic Years

1856–1865

From the end of 1856 till March of 1858 Livingstone was home. He had been parted from wife and children for five long years, and nobody realized more than he did what a burden of anxiety Mrs. Livingstone had carried all that while. One of his greatest sorrows was the death of his father, whom he had longed to see again, but who died during Livingstone's voyage home. The honors bestowed upon him were numberless. He received awards from the cities of Glasgow and Edinburgh, honorary doctorate degrees from Oxford and Cambridge, and a Gold Medal from the Geographical Society. These were only a few of his distinctions. He wrote his book entitled *Missionary Travels* in 1857, and it was a phenomenal success. The simple, direct, unassuming style of the book was a most appropriate clothing for the thoughts and deeds of the man. It may be said that Livingstone's writings were in a marked degree a revelation of his personality and character. You could not read the narrative without wondering at the achievements and conceiving a personal affection for the author.

In all parts of the kingdom, there was extraordinary eagerness to see and hear him. The most distinguished people competed for the honor of entertaining him, the universities showed exceptional enthusiasm while, in humbler places which had associations with his fame, the celebrations were touching in their love and pride. Much of the public laudation was distasteful to him, but he greatly enjoyed the interaction now open to him with men and women of kindred spirit in all churches and among all professions. One problem, in regard to the future, was settled in a characteristic way. Believing, as he did, that it was his life mission to open up this great, newly-discovered land and do pioneer work in the African interior, he felt that he ought to resign his position under the London Missionary Society, as some of its supporters might not approve of this kind of work being undertaken by one of its agents. At the same time, he was exceedingly anxious that the work of the Society should not suffer and regarded it as his own duty to provide a substitute. Accordingly, he arranged with his brother-in-law, Mr. John Moffat, to become a missionary to the Makololo, promising him a sufficient salary for five years.

His own immediate future was determined by the offer from Lord Palmerston of the post of Consul at Quilimane and Commander of an expedition for exploring Eastern and Central Africa. He was to take out a light paddle steamer suitable for the navigation of the Zambezi River, and his colleagues were to include a botanist, mining expert, artist, and ship engineer. This offer was cordially accepted and all arrangements were made for departure.

There will always be some people, the victims of the watertight compartment theory of life, who will hold that a man cannot be a minister or a missionary if he is anything else. These people believe that if a man becomes an explorer he ceases to be a missionary. To be consistent, they ought to believe that when Paul practiced as a tent-maker he ceased to be an apostle, or that a bishop becomes a secular person if he attends to his parliamentary duties. It is needless to say that Livingstone held no such impossible conception of the ministry. He never at any time ceased to be a missionary. All his work was regarded by him as sacred, because it was done for the glory of God and the advancement of Christ's Kingdom. The ends that he pursued till the close of his life were essentially the same that he had sought hitherto—the Kingdom of God and His righteousness.

One of the most impressive addresses delivered by Livingstone during this visit, and one which produced the most lasting effect, was to a distinguished university audience in the Senate House at Cambridge. It was a magnificent and irresistible appeal for missionaries. He was amazed that some of our societies had to go abroad to Germany for missionaries because of the lack of the missionary spirit at home. Livingstone repudiated the talk about sacrifice. He reminded his listeners that no sacrifice was worthy to be mentioned in the same breath as the Great Sacrifice that was made by Christ as He took upon Himself the form of a servant. He closed with this impressive appeal: "I beg to direct your attention to Africa; I know that in a few years I shall be cut off in that country, which is now open: do not let it be shut again! I go back to Africa to try to make an open path for commerce and Christianity; it is for you to carry out the work which I have begun. I leave it with you!"

It was by such glowing words as these that he impressed on British audiences his favorite theme that "the end of the geographical feat is the beginning of the missionary enterprise." Fresh from the ovations and honors which reached their culmination at the grand final banquet in Liverpool, at which foreign statesmen, dukes, earls, bishops, and scientific magnates vied with one another in celebrating his fame, Livingstone sailed from Liverpool on the colonial steamer H.M. *Pearl*. Nothing had been wanting to his success. He was now rich, famous, powerful, and the accredited representative of the respected British Empire. Instead of having to provide for his journeys of exploration out of a meager salary and the generosity of African chiefs, he had the wealth of England behind him and limitless good will. On the deck of the *Pearl* were the sections of the little steam-launch *Ma Robert*, which a philanthropic firm had sold him "as a great bargain for the good of the cause," and which was the most ill-constructed, clumsy, and extravagant vessel that ever ruined the hopes of its owner. Going back with him was his wife and his youngest boy. His brother Charles, too, had been assigned to him as a colleague by a generous Government. One of Livingstone's first acts was to read to the members of the expedition the instructions drawn up by himself with the sanction of the Foreign Office. In these he laid stress on "an example of consistent moral conduct," "treating the people with kindness," "inculcating

> All his work was regarded by him as sacred, because it was done for the glory of God and the advancement of Christ's Kingdom.

peace and good will"; he "earnestly pressed" upon the members "a sacred regard to life" and the avoidance of wanton destruction of animals, and expressed the hope that arms would never be needed for defense against the natives, as "the best security from attack consists in upright conduct." He insists on "the strictest justice in dealing with the natives," and an attitude of respect to the chiefs of tribes. "We are adherents of a benign, holy religion, and may by consistent conduct and wise, patient efforts become the harbingers of peace to a hitherto distracted and downtrodden race." He concluded by again reiterating that "a kind word or deed is never lost."

These instructions are very notable, and perhaps one may read between the lines some anxiety, and even apprehension, for he knew that the success of the expedition no longer entirely rested on himself, and might be marred by ill-advised and unchristian action on the part of any single member. It was well that he could not forecast the future. The years that were to elapse until his return to England in 1864 were in many respects tragic years. They were years of accumulated disappointments, bereavements, failures and rebuffs, faced with courage and borne with resignation, but none the less leaving upon his life the shadow of great and crushing sorrow which never wholly lifted. The course of the *Pearl* was down the West Coast of Africa, and the first bitter disappointment was when his wife and son had to be left behind at Cape Town owing to ill-health. Fortunately, Dr. and Mrs. Moffat had journeyed down to meet them and took their daughter and her boy back to Kuruman. Nevertheless, "it was bitter parting with my wife, like tearing the heart out of one." Livingstone was obliged to do his work in loneliness, but God gave him the grace to bear it.

The *Pearl* reached the mouth of the Zambezi River on May 14, 1858. She was anchored in the "mangrove swamps," a deadly place for fever, and Livingstone insisted on the small launch *Ma Robert* being fitted together immediately, for he feared the consequences to the newcomers if they did not speedily get away to a healthier location. This meant working on Sunday, for which if life can be saved there is sound Scripture warrant; but the order created no small criticism. "It is a pity," writes Livingstone, "that some people cannot see that the true and honest discharge of everyday life is divine service." The next trial was in the resignation of the naval officer, a matter in regard to which Livingstone was fully exonerated by the Foreign Office, but which nonetheless brought home to him the difficulties of his new position. Instead of waiting for a new officer, Livingstone proceeded to run the ship himself. "It was imagined we could not help ourselves," he wrote later, "but I took the task of navigating on myself and have conducted the steamer over 1,600 miles though, as far as my likings go, I would as soon drive a cab in the November fogs in London as be 'skipper' in this hot sun; but I shall go through with it as a duty."

There was some genuine compensation when he reached Tete, as he was hailed with delirious delight by his old Makololo friends, who had never ceased to believe that he would keep his word to them. "The Tete people often taunted us by saying, 'Your Englishman will never return'; but we trusted you, and now we shall sleep." Disease and fighting had thinned their ranks. Thirty had died of smallpox and six had been killed. Livingstone had some work to do before he was ready to march back with the survivors to Linyanti, but they knew he would not fail them. Already it was clear that the *Ma Robert* was almost useless. Livingstone had applied to the Government for a more suitable vessel and had also ordered one on his own account. He had intended to spend a modest sum but eventually he devoted nearly the whole of the profits of his book, some £6,000, to the purchase of the little steamer *Lake Nyassa*, which he specially destined for the lake whose name she bore, but whose waters she never sailed. The Government agreed to the request, but the *Pioneer* did not arrive until early in 1861 and the *Lake Nyassa* a year later; the latter vessel having then to be put together, which occupied many months. There were two years, therefore, to be devoted to what explorations were possible with the aid of the *Ma Robert*—now frivolously called the "Asthmatic"—and their own exertions. It was clear to Livingstone that the Shiré River, a tributary of the Zambezi out of the north country, was a very important feature and ought to be thoroughly examined. It was quite possible that it might prove to be a highway to the inland lakes of which rumor reached him, so the first months of 1859 were devoted to this journey. The party made their way up until they were stopped by cataracts, which were named the Murchison Falls. Little could be done among the natives, who were very suspicious and armed with poisoned arrows. It was necessary constantly to assure them that the expedition was not Portuguese, but British, for the terror of slave raids was like a perpetual nightmare over the people. A second attempt on the Shiré, two months later, had more notable results. They were inspired to strike away from the river to the east and discovered Lake Shirwa. The lake lay 1,800 feet up and was sixty miles long. It is remarkable that the Portuguese had no idea of its existence. Livingstone describes its remarkable beauty and the grandeur of its setting among the mountains, some of which rise to the height of 8,000 feet—"much higher than any you see in Scotland," he writes to his little daughter Agnes. He is increasingly impressed that the whole region is suitable for cotton and sugar. The land is "so rich that the grass towers far over one's head in walking." The party went back to the mouth of the Zambezi for supplies, and then returned to make a determined effort to find Lake Nyassa.

Passing beyond the cataracts, they were assured by a chief that the Shiré River "stretched on for two months, and then came out between perpendicular rocks which could not be passed." "Let us go back to the ship," said the Makololo who were with them, "it is no use trying to find this lake." "We shall see the wonderful rocks, at any rate," said Livingstone. "Yes," they grumbled, "and when you see them you will just want to see something else." However, the curiosity of the Englishmen was by this time thoroughly aroused and they pushed forward till, on the sixteenth of September, they discovered Lake Nyassa. They had no time to do much by way of exploration, and two years were to elapse before Livingstone returned and satisfied himself that the lake was at least two hundred miles long, and that it had endless possibilities in view of future colonization. Even now, however, the slavers were active, and gangs of captives were being marched to the coast, greatly to the indignation of the Makololo. They wondered why Livingstone would not let them "choke" the marauders; but he was occupied with more heroic measures that would lay an ax to the roots of the slave trade. The highlands of the great Shiré waterway, together with the lake stretching two hundred miles to the north, filled his brain with schemes for colonizing the district. It is the best white man's country he has seen, and he bombards his English friends with letters on the subject. Why should honest poor folk at home make a miserable pittance by cultivating small crofts of land when here is a vast undeveloped country waiting for their occupation, with the well-being and safety of a large population to be secured by their presence? He is personally prepared to invest two or three thousand pounds in such an enterprise. "It ought not to be looked on as the last alternative a family can come to, but the performance of an imperative duty to our blood, our country, our religion, and to human kind."

While waiting the response of England to these appeals, he set off with his Makololo for six months, to see them back to their land and their folks. Some have perished, as we have seen; some had no wish to return. About thirty of them deserted before they had gone far, leaving about sixty to go forward. Livingstone's white companions were his brother and Dr. Kirk, afterwards Sir John Kirk, who had proved himself an invaluable friend and comrade.

As for the great traveler himself, it was with real joy that he found himself on the old trail, marching and camping in the fashion so reminiscent of earlier days. There were the same tasks and toils, the same fight with hunger and fatigue and fever; but it cheered his heart: "He rejoiceth as a strong man to run his course." At times, however, he was compelled to realize how hard it is to do good and not do evil with it. He had opened up a path, and the first to follow him was the Portuguese or Arab slave dealer. He felt that he had been made the instrument of the undoing of some innocent people and his heart was heavy. Only Christian settlements could defeat these sinister enterprises. In August, they were at the Victoria Falls and most unexpectedly found a white man there, Mr. Baldwin by name, who had news of a great tragedy that filled Livingstone's soul with sorrow. One of the results of his missionary appeals in England had been that the London Missionary Society had resolved on a mission at Linyanti. Nine Europeans set out for this spot, and Mr. Baldwin had helped them get started. Nevertheless, the head of the mission, Mr. Helmore, and his wife had perished of fever, and three others succumbed later, so that the survivors gave up in alarm and returned. Livingstone was too late to be of service, though he was certain his remedies might have saved their lives. Even this was not all, for Livingstone was told that his old friend Sekelétu was stricken with leprosy and was living away from his people, believing himself to be bewitched. His joy, however, at Livingstone's return was unbounded, and the general happiness did something to make up for the sad news. He was also encouraged to hear that his old friend Sechéle was doing well and happy in the evident satisfaction that Livingstone, British Consul, resumed his old labors of preaching and teaching. It could not be for long, however, for he had to be back on the Zambezi; but he could not neglect any opportunity of doing definitely spiritual work. They reached Tete once more on November 23 and traveled down the river in the *Ma Robert*, the last voyage of that ill-fated "bargain." A month later she grounded on a sandbank and filled with water; without remorse, they left her at the bottom of the Zambezi.

To Livingstone it seemed that 1861 was to mark the opening of a new era, for the long-expected steamer *Pioneer* arrived at the end of January, and with it Bishop Mackenzie and his staff whose object was to plant the "Universities' Mission," another fruit of Livingstone's memorable home visit. Livingstone liked the Bishop from the first for his manly character, his devotion, and his common sense. Differences of denomination affected him not at all. He "looks upon all godly men as good and true brethren." He thought the Bishop was like Dr. Moffat "in his readiness to put his hand to anything."

Some time was lost in exploration of the river Rovuma which came to nothing. Then the navigation of the Shiré with the *Pioneer* proved very slow and laborious because of low water and sandbanks. Worse than all, the whole country seemed to have been ravaged by the slavers, and it was evident that Portuguese Government officials actively conspired in these crimes. At the village of Mbame on the

Shiré, Livingstone and the Bishop liberated a gang of eighty-four
men and women and attached them to the mission settlement. A
peculiarly murderous native chief, the head of a fierce tribe called
the Ajawa, was doing the deadly work for the Portuguese, and when
a visit was paid to him to persuade him to desist, he fired on the
mission party, and the fire was returned. It was an ominous beginning to a noble effort to disrupt the slave traders. It was difficult for
the Bishop and Livingstone to remain spectators to all these murderous onslaughts, but Livingstone strongly advised him not to interfere in tribal quarrels if he could avoid it. A little later the Bishop
returned to the ship and assured Livingstone that the Ajawa were
more peaceably disposed. The latter heard the report, however, with
suspicions that later proved well-founded. The Bishop went back to
his station, and Livingstone's thoughts were turned to the prospec-
tive arrival of the man-of-war that was to bring his own new vessel,
the *Lake Nyassa*, as well as his wife, the Bishop's sister, and some
more members of the mission.

The ship arrived at the end of January 1862, and among
other passengers was the Rev. James Stewart, afterwards so well
known as Dr. Stewart of Lovedale. He had come to represent the
United Free Church of Scotland and survey for a mission station.
The Bishop had not appeared to meet his sister, and boats were
dispatched up river to find him. Miss Mackenzie and Mrs. Burrup,
the wife of one of the Bishop's colleagues, went with the boats.
What they actually found was the well-authenticated story that
the Bishop and Mr. Burrup were dead of fever, after an expedition
to rescue the captive husbands of some Manganja women. The
blow to Livingstone was a crushing one, for though he had never
been able wholly to approve the policy of the mission, he was too
chivalrous to criticize in such an hour and declared that had he
been with the Bishop he would have done the same. "This will
hurt us all," he said prophetically, as the two sorrow-stricken
women came back to Shupanga with the terrible tidings. He knew
well that the Portuguese would misrepresent the object of missionary settlements, that is, to interfere among the tribes and even
to make use of military force, so adding to the mischief instead of

lessening it. "We must bow to the will of Him who doeth all things well," he writes; "but I cannot help feeling sadly disturbed in view of the effect the news may have at home. I shall not swerve a hair's-breadth from my work while life is spared."

Some weeks were spent in arranging for the return of the bereaved women who did not sail for home until April second. Meanwhile, an even darker cloud of sorrow was preparing to break over Livingstone. His wife had only returned to him to die. She had been to Kuruman, where their youngest child was born. Then she had returned to Scotland to see the other children. Nevertheless, her longing to be at her husband's side was intense, and at last she had come back to him. On April 21 she was taken ill with fever, and on the evening of Sunday, the twenty-seventh, in the presence of Dr. Stewart and her husband, she sank to rest. Dr. Stewart tells us how he found Livingstone "sitting by the side of a rude bed formed of boxes, but covered with a soft mattress, on which lay his dying wife." For the first time in his life, Livingstone says he would be content to die. He laid her to rest under a baobab tree[5] on "Shupanga brae" [i.e., hillside]. His diary reveals the agony of his heart. Henceforth "the red hills and white vales" of Shupanga are with him in all his wanderings. "In some other spot I may have looked at, my own resting place may be allotted. I have often wished that it might be in some far-off still deep forest, where I may sleep sweetly till the resurrection morn." "I loved her when I married her, and the longer I lived with her the more I loved her.... Oh! My Mary, my Mary, how often we have longed for a quiet home, since you and I were cast adrift at Kolobeng; surely the removal by a kind Father who knoweth our frame means that He rewarded you by taking you to the best home, the eternal one in the Heavens."

For such comfort as could be obtained in such dark days he turned again to his work. The fight against slavery was becoming more and more desperate as Livingstone was often forced to fire upon slave traders who refused to free their captives. Even the navigation of the river was now a horror. The ghastly waters were strewn with corpses. "The paddles had to be cleared of bodies caught in the floats at night." Human skeletons were found in all

---

[5] Of the bombax family, having a thick trunk, and found in Africa and India; fiber from its bark is used for making rope, paper, etc., and the gourdlike fruit has an edible pulp.

directions. "Many had ended their misery under shady trees, others under projecting crags in the hills, while others lay in their huts with closed doors which, when opened, disclosed the decaying bodies of men, women and children." Eighteen months before, this was a prosperous and highly populated valley; now it is a desert "literally strewn with human bones." To complete his despair, the mission of Bishop Mackenzie was removed, by order, to Zanzibar, despite Livingstone's urgent entreaty; and finally, in July 1863, he himself received from Lord Russell the news that he was recalled. He does not blame the British Government. He has expected this. The bitterness, however, is that "900 miles of coast are abandoned to those who were the first to begin the slave trade, and seem determined to be the last to abandon it."

His instructions as to handing back the *Pioneer* to the Government men were quite explicit, and it was clear that he had little time left to resolve his affairs in Africa. Yet before he returned to England, he accomplished two feats that would have made the reputation of any other man. With only one white colleague and five Makololo, he marched seven hundred and sixty miles in fifty-five days, getting to within ten days' march of Lake Bangweulu, or Bemba, and the village of Ilala, where years later his own heart was to be buried. He would have reached the lake but for the duty of fulfilling his instructions from the Government. The second great feat was on the ocean. He had to face the problem of trying to sell his own admirable little steamer, the Lake Nyassa. She had cost him a fortune and he needed the money. He could have sold her as a slave vessel, but sooner than do that he would sink her in the Indian Ocean. After many adventures he managed to navigate her to Zanzibar, but he could not negotiate a fair price. The one opportunity left was to sail her across the Indian Ocean and sell her in Bombay. It was the wildest adventure, but it was worthy of him. He could take but fourteen tons of coal, and the distance was 2,500 miles. The crew consisted of himself, a stoker, carpenter, sailor, seven native Zanzibarians, and two men—one of whom was Chumah, who was with him on his last march. The voyage took forty-five days, much of it marked by dead calm, but the latter part by furious squalls. The sails were torn, and the little boat nearly rolled right over. Nevertheless, "God's good providence" was "over us," and on June 13, 1864, they crept into the harbor through the fog, their entrance being unobserved. He stayed in Bombay a short time, interesting the merchants in East African trade. Then he departed by ship for England, where he arrived on the twenty-first of July.

The Livingstone who thus returned for his last visit home was in some respects a very altered man from the one who took England by storm at the close of his first great explorations. He had suffered severe personal losses. His wife's death had left him lonely and sad, with the deep and lasting sadness of a strong nature. His grief and disappointment over the tragedy of the Universities' Mission had also left their mark upon him.

Livingstone came back to England in the grip of a great and noble passion to end slavery—a fiery indignation against the barbarities of this traffic in flesh and blood, and he sternly resolved to fight it single-handedly if need be. He had no heart to pursue purely scientific observations or geographical explorations to gratify the intellectuals, while Africa was being desolated and her population laid waste.

Livingstone's return from the second Zambezi expedition in July 1864 must have been a severe disappointment. Not one member of his family came to meet him, and he received none of the fanfare and welcome of his previous return. The aging missionary had lost favor with the press, the clergy, and the British government. His latest trip had created an international incident by exposing the slave trade of the Portuguese. Furthermore, this trip had failed to identify a viable waterway that could open up the African interior to commercial trade and settlement. In short, David Livingstone had made many new enemies during his journey in Africa. As a result of these factors, Livingstone regarded his recall as something of a relief. He

was now unmuzzled; though gentle and kindly as his spirit was, Livingstone was capable of what we may dare to speak of as "the wrath of the Lamb." It becomes more and more evident during this visit that his heart had turned back in full affection to his original vocation and work as a missionary, and when the next negotiations were opened up with him, he bluntly avows his determination to return only on the condition that he may pursue his travels in that capacity. The second experience was, of course, his full contact with all the indescribable villainies of the slave trade. He had seen enough of the miseries it provoked during his journey to Luanda, but the West Coast of Africa was vigilantly watched by English cruisers and the slave trade reduced to comparatively small proportions. On the East Coast, however, Portuguese officials were in authority, and they gladly cooperated with the vast extent of the operations of the raiders. Livingstone came back to England in the grip of a great and noble passion to end slavery—a fiery indignation against the barbarities of this traffic in flesh and blood, and he sternly resolved to fight it single-handedly if need be. He had no heart to pursue purely scientific observations or geographical explorations to gratify the intellectuals, while Africa was being desolated and her population laid waste. The fickle public could not understand why he no longer tickled their ears with thrilling or amusing descriptions of adventures. They had forgotten that he was "a great Puritan traveler," who regarded the moral ends of his labors as the highest priority in life.

With such a fire consuming him, it may easily be realized that he found the Foreign Office "cold." The year was 1864. The United States was in the midst of fighting a terrible civil war, in part due to the nagging evil of slavery on the basis of race. Livingstone's own boy Robert, who had been somewhat eccentric, heard his call and fought in the Federal ranks on his way to a grave in Gettysburg Cemetery. Thousands of volunteers from England, Ireland, and Scotland emigrated to America to help the Federal Army impose its will upon the Confederate States of America. The British government, however, refused to help destroy the Confederate government and chose not to meddle in the War Between the States. The Foreign Office was in no mood to champion the antislavery cause and was, no doubt, heartily relieved that Livingstone had not made a greater fuss about his recall—obviously, he had not come home to complain about his personal affairs. A "fuss" was made, however, about his African friends who were being killed by the thousands, and the rest sold into degradation and forced labor.

He opened his war of words in a lecture to the British Association at Bath. So effective was his opening that the Portuguese had to put up Senhor Lacerda, the traveler, to declare that it was "manifest that Dr. Livingstone, under the pretext of propagating the Word of God, and the advancement of geographical and natural science," was bent on robbing Portugal of the "advantages of the rich commerce of the interior." "Rich commerce" indeed! The learned Senhor goes on to urge that Livingstone's "audacious and mischievous actions" ought to be "restrained." This was a pretty plain hint to the Portuguese authorities, and not lost on them, as we shall see. The next move in the war lay with Livingstone. This was the book in which he proposed to lay the whole scandal bare. He wrote this book at Newstead Abbey, the home of his hospitable friends, Mr. and Mrs. Webb, the former of whom was a noted African hunter.

The day he finished his book was the day when Lincoln was assassinated in Washington.

The book finished, he was asked to respond to a challenge which Sir Roderick Murchison had raised with him, of a return to Africa for purely geographical purposes. Livingstone was eager to return, and the line of exploration suggested on the inland lakes appealed to him strongly, but he answered that he could only feel in the way of duty by working as a missionary. He wrote to Mr. James Young, "I would not consent to go simply as a geographer, but as a missionary, and do geography by the way, because I feel I am in the way of duty when trying either to enlighten these poor people, or open their land to lawful commerce." Later on came an informal request from Lord Palmerston to know what he could do for him. It may be doubted whether that decidedly worldly statesman ever anticipated so disinterested a reply as he received. Instead of bargaining for salary or pension, Livingstone replied that he wanted but one thing; "free access to the highlands by the Zambezi and Shiré [rivers] to be secured by a treaty with Portugal." Governments usually find such men easiest to deal with who are satisfied with a lump sum of money to keep them quiet; Livingstone, however, was unwilling to compromise his vision for an Africa open to the Gospel and opposed to slavery.

In the interval of fixing up his arrangements with the Government and the Royal Geographical Society, Livingstone had a personal sorrow in the death of his mother at the age of eighty-two. He was glad, however, to be at home to fulfill her wish that "one of her laddies should lay her head in the grave." After that, he visited the school which his children attended and made a short speech. The last words he uttered in public in Scotland were the simple ones, "Fear God and work hard."

The negotiations in regard to his new work were finally completed. The Government gave £500, and the Royal Geographical Society an equal sum. A private friend added a thousand pounds. This was all, except that he was to be the unsalaried Consul with power over the chiefs on the coast between Portuguese East Africa (now Mozambique) and Abyssinia (now Ethiopia). He was also warned to expect no pension. It was useless to indulge in belated indignation over these very unhandsome terms; but if they were put into plain black and white these terms meant that the great British Government presented David Livingstone with £500 and a sphere of influence that would keep him from making mischief with the Portuguese by expressing honest British hatred of the slave trade; likewise, the Geographical Society hoped to tie him up with geo-

graphical work and so prevent him from wasting his time and talents on "unprofit-able" missionary en-terprises. What actu-ally happened, we shall see in due course. Meanwhile, Living-stone's own personal plan was to sell his steamer at Bombay in order to raise the ad-ditional funds he needed to finance his new expedition. It was for Bombay, therefore, that he departed in August 1865. He left with the full knowl-edge that he would probably not return to England alive.

An aging David Livingstone with his daughter, Anna Mary, taken in 1864 on his last visit to England.

CHAPTER 7

His Last Great March

1865–1869

When Livingstone arrived in Bombay in September, Sir Bartle Frere was Governor. They were old friends, and the Governor became his very sympathetic host. His immediate purpose was to dispose of the *Lake Nyassa* for what she would fetch. This proved to be £2,600 for a steamer that had cost him £6,000. It was a poor bargain, but he was not in a position to refuse it, and as things turned out he got no good out of it. He deposited the money in an Indian bank which in a few weeks failed miserably, and Livingstone's money was seen no more. Since he cared for money less than any man, he did not allow himself to be unduly depressed by this loss. "The whole of the money she cost," he wrote, "was dedicated to the great cause for which she was built: we are not responsible for results."

His preparations in Bombay for the forthcoming expedition were, for him, quite elaborate and, we may add at once, gave little satisfaction in the field. There was a training school in India for Africans at Nassick. Nine of the men who attended this school volunteered to go with him. Besides these, he was supplied with volunteers from the "Marine Battalion." He was assured that they had been accustomed to roughing it in various ways. In actual reality, these volunteers would only march five miles a day, were "notorious skulkers," and disgusted Livingstone by their cruelty to the brute beasts. It was not long before he dismissed them to their homes. The Nassick men were not much more manageable. The expedition included ten Johanna men who were only a moderate success, two Shupanga men—including Susi—and two Wayaus—including Chumah. Susi and Chumah, it will be remembered, were with him till the last. Chumah was a liberated slave who owed his free-

---

dom to Livingstone and Bishop Mackenzie in 1861. The expedition was further distinguished by a number of animals imported by Livingstone from India: six camels, three buffalo and a calf, two mules, and four donkeys. He was anxious to prove that camels were immune from the bites of the tsetse flies, and he expected to acclimatize the other beasts and teach some native chief to breed them. The Sultan of Zanzibar was cordial and armed Livingstone with a letter to be used as a passport. Then he took his leave, and on the twenty-second of March, he was at the mouth of the Rovuma with all his caravan complete. The navigation of the shallow river proved unexpectedly difficult and occasioned tedious delay and some anxiety. Nevertheless, Livingstone finally managed to sail north again and ultimately land all his animals at Mikindany Bay. He is too experienced a traveler not to realize that his troubles are all in front of him; but he does not anticipate them and writes in high spirits of the joy of setting out once more into wild and unexplored country.

Since David Livingstone was now starting on his last and greatest march, which was to be lengthened out year after year and to be marked by unparalleled sufferings and heroic endurance, it will be well to acquaint ourselves with such plans as he had somewhat vaguely laid down. He realized that there were three great main waterways into the African interior: the Congo, the Zambezi, and the Nile rivers. He was satisfied that no future exploration could do anything other than confirm his conclusions as to the watershed which he had traversed, from which certain rivers flowed north to the Congo, and certain others south to the Zambezi. From earliest times, however, the scientific imagination had been captured by the question of the sources of the Nile. This was the greatest of all unsolved geographical questions, and to it Livingstone was keenly attracted, not only by his own native curiosity, but by that interest in classical questions which was a very marked characteristic of his mind. To this question he knew that the system of inland lakes was the clue, and that whoever could completely explore them would settle the question for all time and "make himself an everlasting name." That he would have numberless opportunities of proclaiming Christ to the scattered peoples of the interior and would cut across the slave routes and perhaps be able to figure out how to defeat the devilish purposes of the slavers, were motives that were even more powerful with him. So he got his caravan under way, marched south to Rovuma, and then southwest across the four hundred miles of country that lay between the coast and Lake Nyassa.

The first stages of the march were made miserable to Livingstone by the brutality of his unqualified volunteers toward the dumb beasts. They were overloaded, overstrained, and cruelly maltreated. Some of them died of sores, which the foolish men insisted were caused by tsetse or by accidents. Meanwhile, progress was depressingly slow; the district through which the expedition passed was famine-stricken, and food was very difficult to obtain. The volunteers ultimately went from bad to worse and in two months were openly mutinous. They killed one camel, beating it over the head, and set themselves to corrupt the Nassick men so as to tire Livingstone out. For weeks on end, it was nothing but one continual struggle on the part of the leader against this conspiracy to defeat his plans. Sometimes he tried the offer of increased wages and, sometimes, the threat of corporal punishment; but the indolence and cruelty of the volunteers threatened the success of the expedition, and the spirit of rebellion spread to the Nassick men.

From earliest times, however, the scientific imagination had been captured by the question of the sources of the Nile. This was the greatest of all unsolved geographical questions, and to it Livingstone was keenly attracted, not only by his own native curiosity, but by that interest in classical questions which was a very marked characteristic of his mind.

On the nineteenth of June, Livingstone made the following journal entry: "We passed a woman tied by the neck to a tree and dead. The people of the country explained that she had been unable to keep up with the other slaves in a gang.... I may mention here that we saw others tied up in a similar manner, and one lying in the path, shot or stabbed, for she was in a pool of blood." They were on the "red trail" now, and Livingstone's feet never left it till death brought him release. On the twenty-seventh of June they found "a number of slaves with slave sticks on, abandoned by their masters from want of food; they were too weak to be able to speak or to say where they had come from. Some were quite young."

The middle of July found them in Mataka's country, with whom Livingstone quickly made friends. The town lay in an elevated valley surrounded by mountains, and food was plentiful so that they were able to make up for many privations. It was here that Livingstone resolved to send the rebellious volunteers back. They had become quite intolerable—shirking work, stealing, and infecting all the company with their ungodly attitudes. One of the incidents that most pleased Livingstone during his stay with Mataka was the release by the chief of a large company of slaves. The expedition left for Lake Nyassa on the twenty-eighth of July. It was mountainous traveling now, but the country between them and the lake was under Mataka, and his guides were sworn to take them safely. Progress was still slow, though decidedly more pleasant in the absence of the former helpers. Sometimes they marched near Arab encampments where the slaves were herded in great pens, from 300 to 800 in a gang, according to Livingstone's estimate. As they drew near the lake, food was plentiful and game abundant. On August 5, "we came to the lake at the confluence of the Misinjé [River], and felt grateful to that Hand which had protected us thus far on our journey. It was as if I had come back to an old home I never expected again to see; and pleasant to bathe in the delicious waters again, hear the roar of the sea, and dash in the rollers.... I feel quite exhilarated." It had taken four months to reach Lake Nyassa from the coast.

Livingstone's plan had been to cross the lake by means of Arab sailboats and resume explorations on the west side; but the Arabs fled from him as from the plague and took every care that no sailboats were at his disposal. As a result, he was forced to march round to the foot of the lake, where he was again on familiar ground. As the veteran missionary marched, he voiced anew his lamentations over the untimely end of the Universities' Mission, which he had always seen in his mind's eye standing sentinel over this great inland sea, and holding the country for Christ and freedom.

The end of September finds the expedition on the Shiré River, and now rumor reaches them of wars and troubles ahead, which causes the Johanna men to desert en masse, and Livingstone does not indulge in many regrets. They had been "inveterate thieves;" but he is left with a party inconveniently small. The sequel to this treachery on the part of the Johanna men was that, to justify themselves, they invented and circulated a most plausible and circumstantial story of Livingstone's murder—a story which reached many of his friends and produced a crop of laudatory obituary notices in the papers. The story was as thoroughly disbelieved by Livingstone's old friend, Mr. E. D. Young, who well knew how the leader of these men could lie. Mr. Young came out to Africa at once, bringing with him a steel boat, the *Search*, which, by the aid of some Makololo men, was successfully transported to Lake Nyassa and floated there. Mr. Young effectually disproved the Johanna legend and in eight months was back again in England, having discovered that Livingstone had passed safely on toward the northwest.

The depleted expedition found itself now in very mountainous regions and enjoyed the noble prospects afforded from many of the high plateaus which they reached. Their faces were to the north, towards the Loangwa River and the distant Lake Tanganyika. No opportunity is lost by the way of preaching to all the tribes "our relationship to our Father; His love for all His children; the guilt of selling any of His children—the consequence: e.g., it begets war, for they don't like to sell their own and steal from other villages who retaliate." Going west from the lake they followed a very zigzag course, crossing many rivers which flow into the Lintipe River which is one of the main supplies of Lake Nyassa. They kept to the north of the fine Zalanyama range, and pushed on in a northwesterly direction. All the while, a state of fear existed in regard to the dreaded Mazitu, who were reported to be making forays, and whom Livingstone compared to the Highland Celts in the twelfth century in the Border country. By the middle of December they had reached the Loangwa and crossed it in search of food. Christmas Day was spent wretchedly, the goats having been stolen and Livingstone's favorite milk-diet was brought to an end. A ridge of mountain country had to be crossed, after which they were compelled to bear to the east in search of food, which had become very scarce again. All the party were suffering. The last day of 1866 is sacred to some new resolutions: "Will try to do better in 1867, and be better—more gentle and loving; and may the Almighty, to Whom I commit my way, bring my desires to pass and prosper me. Let all the sin of '66 be blotted out for Jesus' sake."

> **January 1st, 1867.** — May He who was full of grace and truth impress His character on mine. Grace—eagerness to show favor; truth—truthfulness, sincerity, honor; for His mercy's sake.

The year opened with "a *set-in* rain"—a rain that blows in toward the shore. He recorded that he felt always hungry, and was constantly dreaming of better food when he should be sleeping. On the tenth, he took his belt up three holes to relieve hunger. On the fifteenth, he suffered the loss of his "poor little dog, Chitané," to which he was greatly attached. Everywhere it was famine and famine prices for wretched food. They boiled grain and pretended it was coffee. The ground was all sloppy—feet constantly wet. The natives were living on mushrooms and leaves. Then came the crowning disaster. Two men, who had joined the expedition, deserted and absconded with the medicine chest. It was in the midst of the forest; there was no feasible way of recovering it. There was little doubt that the lack of any proper medicines to counteract the fever poison was a main contributory cause to Livingstone's serious loss of health. "I felt as if I had now received the sentence of death, like poor Bishop Mackenzie," he writes. Yet even in the hour of despair, he searched for some support for optimism and the providential order which he knew to exist. "This may turn out for the best by taking away a source of suspicion among more superstitious, charm-dreading people further north." On January 23, he remarks that "an incessant hunger teases us ... real, lasting hunger and faintness." Yet the next day it was a case of "four hours through unbroken, dark forest," but they had reached the Chambezé, lean and starved and desperate, where there was prospect of food on the other side. They found the food a little later, but "in changing my dress this morning I was frightened at my own emaciation."

The expedition made a lengthy stay with the chief Chitapangwa, who on the whole treated them well and sent men to set Livingstone and his companions on their way to Lake Tanganyika. The same steady tramp, tramp, tramp continued. Always we seem to hear what Dr. Isaac Taylor described as "the forward tread ... which means getting there"; but it was terrible trek. Livingstone had rheumatic fever again; and no medicine! On March 10, he wrote: "I have been ill of fever... every step I take jars in the chest, and I am very weak; I can scarcely keep in the march though formerly I was always first.... I have a constant singing in the ears, and can scarcely hear the loud tick of the chronometers." Still he went on with the rest; at last, on the first day of April, they arrived at Tanganyika, or, as it is called at the southern end, Lake Liemba. It had been good marching under the most trying conditions. The veteran traveler had gone from the south of Lake Nyassa to the south of Lake Tanganyika in six months. Ill as he was, he was deeply impressed by the loveliness of the scenery. Mountains running up to 2,000 feet surrounded the southern portion, "and there, embosomed in tree covered rocks, repose[d] the lake peacefully in the huge cup-shaped cavity." Again he wrote: "It lies in a deep basin whose sides are nearly perpendicular, but covered well with trees; the rocks which appear are bright red argillaceous schist;[6] the trees at present all green; down some of these rocks come beautiful cascades, and buffaloes, elephants, and antelopes wander and graze on the more level spots." It is an enchanted country; but the getting there, in the absence of medicines, nearly killed him. "I feel deeply thankful at having got so far. I am excessively weak and cannot walk without tottering, and have constant singing in the head. *But the Highest will lead me further.*" After a few days spent at the lake, Livingstone's illness assumes a most alarming form. He has "a fit of insensibility," finds himself "floundering outside the hut and

---

[6] Claylike (argillaceous) metamorphic rock (schist) containing parallel layers of flaky minerals, such as mica or talc, and splitting easily into thin, parallel leaves.

unable to get in," and finally falls back heavily on his head. The servants carried him in, but hours passed before he could recognize where he was.

He was a little better a fortnight later and anxious to move on—but to where? He had intended to follow the lake to the northwest, but the road seemed barred by the Mazitu, who were out for plunder. He had heard of Lake Mweru, which lies to the west some two hundred or two hundred and fifty miles. Was it not possible that this lake may be the common source of the Congo and the Nile? This geographical question was most persistent, and he could not be satisfied to leave Lake Mweru unexplored. On the first day's march, he had another fit of lethargy, but this does not constitute an argument for delay. He reached the village of a chief Chitimba, only to find that the country between him and Lake Mweru was the scene of a small war, which would involve "a long detour round the disturbed district." He decided to wait events, which turned out to be a tedious business; but the Arabs were kind to him, and the enforced leisure was probably beneficial. His diary is full of descriptions of the cruelties inflicted by the slave trade. In all, he was detained at Chitimba's village nearly three months and a half.

In his onward march, he visited the famous Nsama, with whom the war had been waged, and was again laid up with illness in that neighborhood. After this, he crossed the Chisera and the Choma and then ascended the highlands between the rivers and the northern part of the lake. It was exhilarating traveling there, for Livingstone was always pleasantly excited by beautiful and hilly scenery which brings back memories of Scotland. Alas! "The long line of slaves and carriers" was a frequent incident in the march. On the eighth of November he reached Lake Mweru, "which seems of goodly size, and is flanked by ranges of mountains on the east and west." There he slept in a fisherman's hut, for the lake abounded in fish—thirty-nine varieties in all, as the fishermen enumerated. The end of November found him at the town of Kazembe, where he met an Arab trader, Muhammed Bogharib, "with an immense number of slaves," who gave him a meal—the first honey and sugar he had tasted for fourteen months—and was useful to him in many ways. The chief also was civil to Livingstone but had been guilty of hateful barbarities, as the mutilated arms and ears of many of his people bore witness. Livingstone looked with disgust on the executioner who carried sword and scissors for his horrible work. The people generally were more savage than any he had seen.

The results of extended explorations of Lake Mweru, lasting for some months, were set forth in a dispatch to Lord Clarendon, dated the tenth of December 1867. From this dispatch we can see that Livingstone had been misled by a similarity of name to imagine that Lake Bemba, of which he had heard years before, was the same as Lake Liemba. He now knew (1) that Lake Liemba was only the southern portion of Lake Tanganyika; (2) that Lake Bemba was the lake otherwise called Lake Bangweulu; and (3) that on his northern travels from Lake Nyassa, when he crossed the Chambezé River, he had been less than one hundred miles from this latter lake and might have saved himself many miles of trudging had he explored it first of all. He had discovered also that a great river, the Luapula, flows from Lake Bangweulu into the south of Lake Mweru and that, at the north, the waters flow out in what is called the Lualaba River. He was uncertain in his own mind what this great river Lualaba was and where it went. It may be the Nile; it seems more probable that it is the Congo. It may flow into the northern portion of Lake Tanganyika, or it may flow away to the northwest. Livingstone was assured by the natives that Lake Bangweulu was only ten days distant; but he noted, "I am so tired of exploration without a word from home or anywhere else for two years, that I must go to Ujiji on Tanganyika for letters before doing anything else. Besides, there is another reason—I have no medicine." He was satirical on the subject of the published maps, one of which tacked on two hundred miles to Lake Nyassa, and another made a river—"the new Zambezi"—flow four thousand feet uphill! "I have walked over both these locations and did not know that I was walking on water till I saw them in the maps."

The year 1868 found him still interested in Lake Mweru. His New Year's prayer was: "If I am to die this year, prepare me for it." It was towards the end of March that the idea of going south to explore Lake Bangweulu took hold on him. His reason was that he must stay at least two more months at Lake Mweru before a passage could be made to Ujiji. There were many difficulties in the way, notably that his supplies were nearly gone and he could not give presents to chiefs on the way. What was more serious was that those on whose help he counted were in open revolt against his plan. Muhammed Bogharib, who intended to accompany him to Ujiji, was incensed at Livingstone for making a proposal so mad; and the latter expressed the fear that he must give up Lake Bangweulu for the present. The next day, however, he was bent on going, but his own carriers had been corrupted by the Arabs and refused to accompany him. Only five of his men remained loyal, but Livingstone's blood was up now, so he started out at the head of this meager escort to find Lake Bemba or Bangweulu. "I did not blame them very severely in my own mind for absconding," he wrote; "they were tired of tramping, and so verily am I." They might well have resented Livingstone's decision for, at the time, it was understood they were at the north end of Lake Mweru; from there Livingstone went to look at Lualaba, examine the country, and draw his conclusions as to whether this great river was the Congo or the Nile. The way to Tanganyika and Ujiji was now open, and this sudden turn south was almost more than flesh and blood could stand. The leader was immovable, however, and, early in May with his faithful few, he was back at Kazembe's to the south of Lake Mweru, with his mind fully made up for Bangweulu. Again there were tedious delays, and it was the second week in June before he was definitely off for the south. A month's traveling brought him to Lake Bangweulu. A Babisa traveler asked him why he had come so far, and he answered that he wished to make the country and people better known to the rest of the world; that we were all children of one Father, and that he was anxious that we should know each other better, and that friendly visits should be made in safety. He began exploring the islands of the lake. It was bitterly cold on one of them, and the shed where he slept was decidedly airy, but he tells us that he was soon asleep and dreamed that he had accommodations in a first-rate hotel!

At the end of July he started back, and at Kizinga he deviated from his former route and struck out to the north for the Kalongosi River. All went well, and by the first of November he was back again at the north of Mweru, preparing to march to Ujiji, and intently preoccupied with the question of the Nile. The men who had deserted him when he went south were now pleading to be taken back. He reflected that "more enlightened people often take advantage of men in similar circumstances," and added characteristically, "I have faults myself." So all the runaways were reinstated.

> He was fighting the slave trade single-handedly and was surrounded by cruel and unscrupulous enemies whose dark deeds had only him to fear. He was almost beaten in the unequal strife; almost, but never quite. No man is ever totally beaten who is as sure of Christ as he was.

The expedition would have departed without further delay but that the slave raids of Muhammed Bogharib's men stirred up the countryside against him, and Livingstone found himself at the very center of a small war and literally in the zone of fire. Stockades were hastily erected, and the perpetrators of the outrage had to stand a siege. Horrible scenes were witnessed, and Livingstone commented on the miseries which this devilish traffic entailed. The country was now very disturbed and unsafe, and it was not until December 11 that a start could be made.

Mr. Waller described the "motley group" that now set out for Tanganyika: "Muhammed and his friends, a gang of Unyamwezi hangers-on, and strings of wretched slaves yoked together in their heavy slave sticks. Some carry ivory, others copper or food for the march, whilst hope and fear, misery and villainy, may be read off the various faces." Livingstone was now an actual eyewitness of a slave march. The slaves constantly escaped. Sickness and accidents pursued the miserable cavalcade and made progress slow. Food for so many mouths was difficult to obtain. Christmas Day passed in a land of scarcity. The weather was very damp and cheerless; and on New Year's Day, Livingstone got wet through once too often.

Livingstone being carried on a makeshift litter.

Yet he was so anxious to be on the far side of the Lofuko that he waded through, though it was waist deep and very cold. This was the last straw. He broke down utterly, and later wrote that he became "very ill all over; cannot walk; pneumonia of right lung, and I cough all day and all night; sputa[7] rust of iron, and bloody; distressing weakness." He chronicled the illusions that came and went, visualizing himself lying dead on the way to Ujiji and all the letters that awaited him being useless. It seemed as if he was near the end. Muhammed Bogharib constructed a kind of litter for the helpless veteran, and in this litter he was carried forward four hours a day. It was the best that could be done; and yet Livingstone tells of the pain he endured as he was jolted along, sometimes through steep ravines and sometimes over volcanic tuff (porous rock), the feet of the carriers being at times hurt with thorns, and the sun beating down on his face and head, which in his weakness he could not even shelter with a bunch of leaves. For six endless weeks, the sufferer was borne onward in this manner; and on the fourteenth of February all that was left of him was deposited on the shore of

---

[7] Sputa is the plural of sputum—a term derived from Latin [sputus, to spit] and refers to saliva mixed with phlegm that is expectorated from the lungs and respiratory passages.

Lake Tanganyika, and canoes were sought to transport the party up the lake to Ujiji. It was stormy weather on the lake, and the canoes had to creep along the western shore from village to village. "Patience was never needed more than now," wrote the sick man in his extremity—then across the lake to the east, and at last, March 14, the heroic traveler reached his goal and did actually stand for the first time in the streets of Ujiji.

He had fixed so many hopes on this Arab settlement and had lived for so long on the anticipation of letters and journals, supplies, and medicines, that the disappointment awaiting him was heartrending. He had reached a den of thieves, the vilest he had ever known. His supplies were plundered—only eighteen pieces of cloth out of eighty remained and, what was harder to bear, only one old letter out of all that had been sent to him. As for the medicines, he was told they were at Unyanyembe, thirteen days to the east. He knew quite well that there was a conspiracy to thwart him and, if possible, to drive him out of the country or hasten his death. He was fighting the slave trade single-handedly and was surrounded by cruel and unscrupulous enemies whose dark deeds had only him to fear. He was almost beaten in the unequal strife; almost, but never quite. No man is ever totally beaten who is as sure of Christ as he was. He had one thing to rely on, as he said before, "the word of a Gentleman of the strictest honor"—and it was enough. So he would remain and outwit the slave traders if he could. And yet it was a misnomer to call it a "trade"; "it is not a trade, but a system of consecutive murders."

He did not know, though he suspected, how helpless he was in the hands of the Arabs. His bitter cry could not reach England. Forty letters he wrote and paid handsomely for their delivery, but the Arabs took care they should never reach the coast. He was literally cut off in the interior. He heard nothing from Europe, and Europe heard nothing of him. A few weeks at Ujiji were enough. Then, all unfit as he was, he started out again for the country in the northwest, the land of the Manyuema and the great river Lualaba, the direction of which it was his main purpose now to determine. He still believed it was the Nile.

Then, all unfit as he was, he started out again for the country in the northwest, the land of the Manyuema and the great river Lualaba, the direction of which it was his main purpose now to determine. He still believed it was the Nile.

CHAPTER 8

At Death's Door

1869–1871

When Livingstone crossed Tanganyika, heading to the west, and disappeared into the new country, he certainly did not propose to himself more than an eight or nine months' absence. In reality, he left Ujiji on July 12, 1869, and saw it no more until October 23, 1871. For two years and a quarter he wandered on while the civilized world believed him to be dead; and, perhaps, if we had to name one period of his life which was more poignant and more fruitful than any other, it was this. For out of its agonies, a new hope was born for humanity. His health returned somewhat as he went on, though many signs reminded him that he was not the man he used to be. He was only fifty-six, but he was worn out with hardship and privation. He could not walk uphill without panting for breath. His cheeks were hollow, and his teeth were broken or had fallen out from trying to masticate hard and sticky food. "If you expect a kiss from me," he writes to his daughter Agnes, "you must take it through a speaking trumpet!"

The twenty-first of September found him at Bambarré, the capital of the Manyuema country, noting with thankfulness that as he persevered his strength increased. In front of him was the Luamo River, flowing west to its confluence with the Lualaba, which again was not far in distance. He might have fulfilled his ambition to navigate the Lualaba now but could not get any canoe—"all are our enemies"—and so returned reluctantly to Bambarré. It was from Bambarré that he wrote two letters; they were probably posted months later, which actually got through the Arab cordon and eventually reached their owners. One was to his son Tom. He told of his hopes to go down the Lualaba, but he had frightful ulcers on his feet "from wading in mud." Another to

Sir Thomas Maclear, which was more explicit as to his plans, states: "I have to go down and see where the two arms unite—the lost city Meroe ought to be there—then get back to Ujiji to get a supply of goods which I have ordered from Zanzibar, as I finish up by going outside and south of all the sources, so that I may be sure none will cut me out and say he found other sources south of mine.... I have still a seriously long task before me."

> "In this journey I have endeavored to follow with unswerving fidelity the line of duty. All the hardship, hunger, and toil were met with the full conviction that I was right in persevering to make a complete work of the exploration of the sources of the Nile. The prospect of death in pursuing what I knew to be right did not make me veer to one side or the other."

After Christmas, he went away to the north and discovered the Chanya range. Marching through rank jungle and suffering much from fever and "choleraic symptoms,"[8] he turned south again and on the seventh of February went into winter quarters at Mamohela. Muhammed was still with him but went off at this stage in search of ivory. The entries in his diary were now few, but on June 26 the winter season was evidently over, and he proposed to start once again for the Lualaba. Once more, however, he had to reckon with a revolt of his men, who deserted, with the exception of three, among whom were the ever-faithful Susi and Chumah. The path this time was to the northwest. It was difficult and hazardous, but the situation was relieved by the timely arrival of Muhammed Bogharib. It was well, for Livingstone was at the end of his strength. "Flooded rivers, breast and neck deep, had to be crossed, and the mud was awful." His feet "failed him" for the first time in his life. "Irritable, eating ulcers fastened on both feet." In indescribable pain, he "limped back to Bambarré." This was on July 22, 1870.

For the next eighty days he was a prisoner in his hut. He could

---

[8] Cholera is a disease of the small intestines caused by bacteria; its symptoms include excessive watery diarrhea, vomiting, muscle cramps, severe dehydration, and depletion of electrolytes.

do nothing but think, read the Bible, and pray. He read the Bible through four times during his stay in the Manyuema country. He was fascinated by the personality of Moses and his connection with the Nile and thought favorably of the legend that associates him with the lost city, Meroe, at the junction of the two rivers Lualaba. He meditated tenderly on the stratagem of the "old Nile" hiding its head so cunningly and baffling so many human efforts. One of his resources was the Soko, a kind of gorilla, often made captive. It was physically repulsive to him, but it interested him as a naturalist; and later on he became an owner of one, which he domesticates and proposed to take back to Europe. When most helpless, he sketched out his future and, in his imagination, named certain lakes and rivers after old English friends and benefactors—Palmerston, Webb, and Young—and one lake after Abraham Lincoln. On the tenth of October, he was able for the first time to crawl out of his hut. On the twenty-fifth, he made this significant entry in his journal: "In this journey I have endeavored to follow with unswerving fidelity the line of duty. All the hardship, hunger, and toil were met with the full conviction that I was right in persevering to make a complete work of the exploration of the sources of the Nile. The prospect of death in pursuing what I knew to be right did not make me veer to one side or the other." Never had any man a better right to use such words.

He was waiting now for the arrival of Syde bin Habib, Dugumbé, and others who were bringing him letters and medicines from Ujiji. Months passed and there was no sign of them. He was heartsick and weary with the intolerable delay. The one excitement was in the shedding of blood. Every day had its story of horrors, and he could bear it no longer. There were darker tragedies, however, yet to occur before he escaped out of Manyuema country. The year 1871 finally dawned. "O Father! Help me to finish this work to Thy glory."

It was February before the men arrived who were bringing letters and supplies for him; but, alas! "only one letter reached, and forty are missing." The men, too, had been corrupted by the Arabs and refused to go North with him. He was again outwitted by his cunning foes. Weary days of bargaining followed, and at last terms were arranged. The expedition started, and on March 29 Livingstone was at Nyangwé on the bank of the Lualaba, the furthest point westward that he was to reach at that time. He found the Lualaba here "a mighty river 3,000 yards broad."

Livingstone was to learn to his regret that the men who had been sent up country to him—ostensibly to help him on his way— were his worst enemies. They poisoned the minds of the Manyuema against him. They stirred up strife and were guilty of every kind of crime. All Livingstone's efforts to get canoes for exploring the river were neutralized by them; though he afterwards saw in this the hand of God for his deliverance, for these canoes were lost in the rapids. "We don't always know the dangers we are guided past."

We now reach the event which was the climax of Livingstone's moral sufferings, and which, when known in Europe, sent a thrill of horror through the nations which had heard of the lesser agonies of the slave traffic with comparative indifference. On the twenty-eighth of June, one of Syde bin Habib's slaves, named Manilla, set fire to eight or ten villages, alleging an old debt by way of an excuse. He then made blood brotherhood with other tribes, which angered Dugumbé and his followers, who planned revenge. The fifteenth of July was a lovely summer day, and about 1,500 people came together for the market. Livingstone was strolling round observing the life in the marketplace, when three of Dugumbé's men opened fire upon the assembled crowd, and another small troop began to shoot down the panic-stricken women as they fled to the canoes on the river. So many canoes were pushed off at once down the creek that they got jammed, and the murderers on the bank poured volley after volley into them. Numbers of the victims sprang into the water and swam out into the river. Many were hit and sank; others were drowned. Canoes capsized and their occupants were lost. The Arabs reckoned the dead at four hundred, and even then the men who had tasted blood continued the awful butchery and fired village after village. "No one will ever know," writes Livingstone, "the exact loss on this bright, sultry, summer morning; it gave me the impression of being in hell." Dugumbé protested his innocence, and helped to save some who were drowning, but it was clear that Livingstone in his heart accuses him of complicity. He counted twelve burning villages and, on the next day, saw as many as seventeen. "The open murder perpetrated on hundreds of unsuspecting women fills me with unspeakable horror." It "felt to me like Gehenna," he wrote later, and the nightmare never left him afterwards. "I cannot stay here in agony," he added; on the twentieth he started back for Ujiji, in spite of the entreaties of those who had every reason to desire that he should not go away and publish the story. The atrocious wickedness of the Arabs was that they demoralized their slaves and trained them to perpetrate the butchering of other natives, and then excused themselves on the grounds that they had nothing to do with the crime.

The homeward march lay through miles of villages, all burned; it was impossible to convince the wretched survivors that Livingstone himself had not been guilty. Ambushes were laid to murder him and his party. A large spear "almost grazed my back." Another spear missed him by only a foot. Two of his men were slain. A huge tree had been loosened at the roots and almost fell upon him. Three times in one day he escaped death by a hair's-breadth. So impressed were his people that they cried, "Peace! peace! you will finish your work in spite of everything." He took it as a prophetic sign and gave thanks to the "Almighty Preserver of men." For five hours he ran the gauntlet, "perfectly indifferent whether [he] were killed or not."

The march was pursued in great suffering through August and September and on into October. Once, he said, he felt like dying on his feet. He was profoundly shaken and depressed. The infamous traders succeeded, but he had failed, he alone, "and experienced worry, thwarting, baffling, when almost in sight of the end for which [he] strained."

On the twenty-third of October, reduced to a skeleton, "a mere ruckle of bones," he arrived at Ujiji. Shereef who had custody of his goods had sold them all off. Shereef, says Livingstone, is "a moral idiot." Little wonder that he feels like the man in the parable who fell among thieves, only, alas! there was no Good Samaritan. So he felt, but this time he was mistaken. "When my spirits were at their lowest ebb, the Good Samaritan was close at hand." No part of his amazing story is better known. On the morning of October 28, 1871, Susi came running to him "at the top of his speed and gasped out, 'an Englishman. I see him!'"

A caravan was approaching with the American flag flying over it. In a few minutes, the stranger was in front of him holding out his hand with the words, "Dr. Livingstone, I presume!" It was Henry Morton Stanley who had undertaken to find him—alive or dead. He had engaged to do so two years before, and he had kept his word.

CHAPTER 9

The Good Samaritan

1871–1872

In the middle of October 1869, when Livingstone was at Bambarré in search of the Lualaba, Mr. Stanley was traveling from Madrid to Paris in response to an urgent telegram from Mr. James Gordon Bennett, Jr., of the *New York Herald*. "Where do you think Livingstone is?" was Mr. Bennett's query when Stanley arrived. The latter confessed his ignorance. The world in general seemed to be content to go on, regardless of Livingstone's circumstances. Nobody knew for certain whether he was alive or dead. Mr. Bennett approached the question as a journalist. To find Livingstone was the most sensational feat that could be performed. Mr. Bennett probably underrated his own motive of humanity, but he felt that David Livingstone was good "copy," and that if he were discovered, the world would ring with the enterprise of the great paper with which he was honorably associated. His instructions to Mr. Stanley were very simple: "Spare no expense; spend all the money you want; only find Livingstone."

By a curious arrangement, Stanley was first of all to make a grand tour through Constantinople, Palestine, Egypt, and India.

Henry Morton Stanley

That is why he did not cross to Zanzibar till the beginning of 1871. Livingstone might have reappeared in the interval, but there was no sign of him. Accordingly, Stanley organized an imposing expedition of nearly two hundred persons in five caravans, with all kinds of stores, necessary and luxurious, and made for the interior by way of Unyanyembe. There he himself all but perished of fever, and afterwards escaped by a hand's-breadth being made the victim of a war between the Arabs and the natives. However, he stuck to his errand and, as we have seen, arrived in Ujiji and greeted Livingstone just when the latter was most in need of the kind of cheer and aid that Stanley had brought.

Five years had passed since Livingstone had had news of the outer world, and even now it is a question whether Stanley's story to Livingstone or Livingstone's to Stanley was the greater tale. Stanley brought news of the Franco-German War, of General Grant's presidency, of the electric cables laid, and, what touched Livingstone deeply, of a vote of £1,000 for supplies to him by the British Government. So he was not entirely forgotten! Livingstone's story was told by degrees—a story of which Stanley could be left to estimate the heroism and miraculous endurance. Never before or since has such a story of one lone man's achievement been told to any listener. This was the man Stanley had found, this was the man he was now to save from despair and collapse. "You have brought me new life!" Livingstone kept saying, and it was true in every sense. For Stanley had brought him news, food, medicine, comfort, and, above all, companionship. His recovery was remarkable. He began to enjoy every luxury provided for him. He reveled in the descriptions of the history of the memorable five years as Stanley described it in graphic fashion. He read and reread his home letters. He luxuriated in clothes, new and clean and warm. The imagination loves to dwell on this oasis in the desert of his last years. He was supremely happy, full of laughter and anecdote, above all, full of gratitude to the resourceful and admiring friend who had dropped from the clouds to relieve his solitude and brace his soul for the final exploits. It was Stanley's own testimony that this meeting and the cheerful days that followed seemed to take ten years off Livingstone's age and bring back the air of youth to his face and figure.

They planned together an exploration of the northern end of Lake Tanganyika. It was a "picnic," or so Livingstone called it,

In a few minutes, the stranger was in front of him holding out his hand with the words, "Dr. Livingstone, I presume!" It was Henry Morton Stanley who had undertaken to find him—alive or dead. He had engaged to do so two years before, and he had kept his word.

and it was carried out in that spirit. The old explorer had always been convinced that Lake Tanganyika contributed its waters to the Nile. They found but one river at the northern end, and that river flowed *in*, not *out*. Even so, he was not wholly convinced that his theory was unsound. There were incidents in the journey

that revealed to the younger man Livingstone's patience and for-
bearance and the secret of his unique power in gentleness and the
forgiving spirit. The impression made was never effaced.

Of the picture of Livingstone, drawn by Mr. Stanley's sympathetic and accomplished hand, we shall have more to say in
the final chapter. Meanwhile we only record that Stanley succeeded beyond all hopes in the first part of his mission, and as
conspicuously failed in the second. The first part was to find
Livingstone and minister to his needs. There is no manner of
doubt that this mission was well and truly performed. Stanley's
repeated acts of generosity brought tears to Livingstone's eyes,
and this "cold northerner," as he called himself, was moved beyond words. From Stanley he also received an abundance of supplies and medicines, as well as a company of carriers sent back to
him eventually from Zanzibar.

As to the second part of the mission, however, which was to
persuade Livingstone to go home at once—where honors and fortune awaited him, and his nearest and dearest were yearning to see
him again—in this, Stanley had no success. To return and go wea-
rily over many of his old tracks; to dare once again the perils of
fever, the enmity of the slave trader, and the ignorant antagonism
of savage peoples—this was the alternative program, and he was
resolute to carry it out. His question was not yet fully solved, and,
if he could help it, he would not carry mere half-baked theories
back to England after five years of wandering and exile.

When his daughter Agnes wrote, "Much as I wish you to
come home, I had rather that you finished your work to your own
satisfaction than return merely to gratify me," he writes proudly
in his journal: "Rightly and nobly said, my darling Nannie; vanity
whispers pretty loudly, 'She is a chip off the old block.' My blessing on her, and all the rest."

The plan then formed between the two travelers was to return together to Unyanyembe where Stanley had supplies waiting. The latter would then push on rapidly to Zanzibar and send
back carriers for Livingstone's new expedition. With these, the
veteran proposed to return to a final examination of the sources

of the great rivers, clear up the points still in dispute, and then turn his face home. They set out together at the end of the year 1871 and arrived after seven weeks' traveling at Unyanyembe on February 18, 1872. The march is prosaically recorded by Livingstone. The most frequent entries concern Stanley's repeated attacks of fever. Occasionally he was so weak that he had to be carried. Were it not for the tireless ministration of his great companion and the cheering effect of his presence, which was worth many doses of quinine, Stanley might easily have succumbed. They reached their destination only to find that thieves had been active as usual, and that both Livingstone's and Stanley's supplies had been extensively plundered. There was enough left, however, to make Livingstone feel rich: "I am quite set up; and as soon as he can send me men, not slaves, from the coast, I go to my work, with a fair prospect of finishing it."

> As to the second part of the mission, however, which was to persuade Livingstone to go home at once—where honors and fortune awaited him, and his nearest and dearest were yearning to see him again—in this, Stanley had no success. To return and go wearily over many of his old tracks; to dare once again the perils of fever, the enmity of the slave trader, and the ignorant antagonism of savage peoples— this was the alternative program, and he was resolute to carry it out. His question was not yet fully solved, and, if he could help it, he would not carry mere half-baked theories back to England after five years of wandering and exile.

The two friends remained together nearly a month at Unyanyembe. Letters and parcels arrived. Livingstone rejoiced in "four flannel shirts from Agnes," and "two pairs of fine English boots" from a friend. Dispatches have to be written, articles for the *New York Herald*, and grateful letters to many American and English friends—all of which Stanley will take with him. At last, on March 14, the time has come to say good-bye. Livingstone's entry in his diary is characteristic: "Mr. Stanley leaves. I commit to his care my journal, sealed with five seals; the impressions on them are those of an American gold coin, anna[9] and half anna, and cake of paint with royal arms. Positively not to be opened." All that one man (naturally reticent and reserved) could say of the limitless kindness shown by Stanley and the noble interest taken by America, Livingstone expressed in his private letters. It is to Stanley's picturesque pen that we owe the description of the final parting, and we may well quote a few sentences from it: "My days seem to have been spent in an Elysian field;[10] otherwise, why should I so keenly regret the near approach of the parting hour? Have I not been battered by successive fevers prostrate with agony day after day lately? Have I not raved and stormed in madness? Have I not clenched my fists in fury, and fought with the wild strength of despair when in delirium? Yet I regret to surrender the pleasure I have felt in this man's society, though so dearly purchased...."

> **March 14th.**—We had a sad breakfast together. I could not eat, my heart was too full; neither did my companion seem to have an appetite. We found something to do which kept us longer together. At eight o'clock I was not gone, and I had thought to have been off at 5:00 a.m."; but the final parting had to be faced. The Doctor walked out a little way with his friend, and started him on his journey. The carriers were in a lively mood, singing on the march. The two friends walked side by side, Stanley searching Livingstone's features to impress every detail on his memory. At last he halted. "Now, my dear Doctor, the best friends must part; you have come far enough, let me beg of you to turn back." "Well," Livingstone replied, "I will say this of you: you have done what few men could do—far better than some great travelers I know. And I am grateful to you for what you have done for me. God guide you safe home and bless you, my friend." "And may God bring you safe back to us all, my dear friend. Farewell!" "Farewell!"

---

[9] A former monetary unit of India and Pakistan which was equal to 1/16 of a rupee.
[10] Taken from Greek mythology and refers to a place or condition of ideal happiness.

Livingstone turned away. Did his heart forebode that this was the last white face he would ever see, the last white hand he would ever press? Did he feel that he was turning his back forever on home, and rest, and freedom? Just when a dip in the path would hide the returning exile finally from view, Stanley turned to take one more look. "The old man in grey clothes was still there. He, too, turned round. He was standing near the gate of Kwihaha with his servants near him. I waved a handkerchief to him, and he responded by lifting his cap."

This was on the fourteenth of March. On March 27, at a spot agreed upon, Susi and Hamaydah found Stanley and delivered to him a letter, signed by Livingstone, in which the latter gave this well-seasoned Scottish counsel, "to put a stout heart to a stey brae [i.e., a steep hillside]"; rejoiced that Stanley's fever has assumed "the intermittent or safe form"; and concluded, "I feel comfortable in commending you to the guardianship of the good Lord and Father of all."

Two days later it was Livingstone's birthday, and his diary reminds us that though this new friend had come and gone, there was One Who was with him always even to the end of the world.

March 19th. — My birthday. My Jesus, my King, my Life, my all! I again dedicate my whole self to Thee. Accept me. And grant, O Gracious Father, that ere this year is gone I may finish my work. In Jesus' name, I ask it. Amen.

While he was lying on his litter outside and the rain
was falling, curious villagers had gathered round,
each man with bow in hand, for they had
been guarding their crops.
This was the great chief who had come from far.
His fame they knew somewhat; they could not know
that he was the best friend Africa ever had.

CHAPTER 10

His Final Days

1872–1873

As we have seen, Livingstone said farewell to Stanley on March 14, 1872, and prepared to wait in Unyanyembe until his friend had reached Zanzibar and sent a body of picked natives back to act as his escort. In his diary he made careful reckonings as to the length of time this meant and concluded that he could not expect his men until July 15. It was August 14 before they arrived. He had to wait five weary months at Unyanyembe, and the lateness of his start brought the wet weather near and handicapped the expedition from the first. We may just say for the record that Stanley's march to the coast was beset with difficulties—"the whole ten plagues of Egypt"—but it was successfully accomplished, and the men he sent back to Livingstone were of the very best. Stanley encountered at Zanzibar members of an English relief expedition that had been sent out to find and assist Livingstone. Of this expedition, the explorer's son Oswell was a member. After hearing Stanley's news they decided that it was unnecessary to go on, and returned to England.

To the ordinary person, five months of waiting would have been almost intolerable. There were signs that even Livingstone had some ado to sit still and count the days. Nevertheless, if they were profitless months to him, and if often he was, as he records, "weary, weary," the revelations contained in his journal were by no means profitless to us. He had time to write fully as to his plans and his motives. He takes us into his confidence and we see that he had lost nothing in all these years of that eager curiosity which belonged to him as a boy. He still carried in his breast "the heart of a little child." The wonderful Ptolemy[11] and the naive Herodotus[12] were pondered

---

[11] A mathematician, astronomer, and geographer from Alexandria, Egypt.
[12] An historian from Greece.

over; all the stories of "fountains" and "pillars" were awakened in the great traveler the desire to test them for himself. He was evidently not sure that there was not something in them after all. He dearly wanted to find out. He could not reconcile Ptolemy with the investigation of Baker, Speke, and Grant,[13] and it had all the delight of a fascinating conundrum to him.

> "All I can add in my loneliness is, may Heaven's rich blessing come down on everyone—American, English, or Turk—who will help to heal the open sore of the world."

April 18th. — I pray the good Lord of all to favor me so as to allow me to discover the ancient fountains of Herodotus, and if there is anything in the underground excavations to confirm the precious old documents (ta biblia) the Scriptures of truth, may He permit me to bring it to light, and give me wisdom to make a proper use of it.

On the first of May, he recorded that he had finished a letter to the *New York Herald.* This was the letter which concluded with the now world-renowned words upon his tablet in Westminster Abbey—"All I can add in my loneliness is, may Heaven's rich blessing come down on everyone—American, English, or Turk—who will help to heal the open sore of the world." Providentially, the words were written one year to the very day before the writer's death.

He meditated much on the native faiths. He recognized as the fundamental fact "dependence on a Divine Power," but "without any conscious feeling of its nature." He noted also their belief in a continued existence after death, so as to be able to do good to those they love and evil to those they hate. "I don't know how the great loving Father will bring all out right at last, but He knows and will do it." For himself, his confidence was anchored, as it had always been, in the plain word of Christ, the perfect Gentleman.

May 13th. — He will keep His word, the Gracious One, full of grace and truth—no doubt of it. He said, "Him that cometh unto Me, I will in no wise cast out," and "Whatsoever ye shall ask in My name that will I do." He will keep His word: then I can come

---

[13] Sir Samuel W. Baker, Captain John Hanning Speke, and Captain Grant, all of whom made expeditions into the interior of Africa and documented their travels.

and humbly present my petition and it will be all right. Doubt is here inadmissible, surely.

He read Speke's travels with critical enjoyment and spent a page or two in challenging his statement that African mothers sell their own children. He did not believe it. He had never known an instance, nor had the Arabs. He always defended the positive qualities of the natives and their common human feelings. Then he appealed to the heroism of the Church at home to come and help the African people. "I would say to missionaries, Come on, brethren, to the real heathen. You have no idea how brave you are till you try. Leaving the coast tribes and devoting yourselves heartily to the savages, as they are called, you will find, with some drawbacks and wickednesses, a very great deal to admire and love." A little later, he argued that the interior is a tempting field for "well-sustained efforts of private benevolence." He thought the missionary should make up his mind not to depend upon "foreign support," and gave instances of his own resourcefulness where he had none to depend on but himself. He was for "a sort of Robinson Crusoe life," the great object being "to improve the improvable among the natives." As to method, he wrote later, "no jugglery or sleight of hand … would have any effect in the civilization of Africans; they have too much good sense for that. Nothing brings them to place thorough confidence in Europeans but a long course of well-doing.… Goodness and unselfishness impress their minds more than any kind of skill or power. They say, 'You have different hearts from ours.'… The prayer to Jesus for a new heart and a right spirit at once commends itself as appropriate." He noted, too, that music influenced them and often led to conversion.

Scattered through the journal are his usual keen observations on the animal and plant life of the district, together with brief narratives of tribal quarrels and crimes. Again and again he confessed uncertainty as to whether he had not been tracing the sources of the Congo rather than the Nile. If he had not had a scientific mind and training, he argued that long before this he would have cried "Eureka!" and gone home with a half-proved hypothesis;

but his absolute love of truth forbade it.

By the middle of July his men had not yet come, though he had heard that they were on the way. He was very tired of the delay but returned at length to the subject of missions in Africa and indulged in one passage, clearly showing that his Puritan common sense never deserted him:

> A couple of Europeans beginning and carrying on a mission without a staff of foreign attendants implies coarse country fare, it is true, but this would be nothing to those who at home amuse themselves with fasts, vigils, etc. A great deal of power is thus lost in the church. Fastings and vigils, without a special object in view, are time run to waste. They are made to minister to a sort of self-gratification, instead of being turned to account for the good of others. They are like groaning in sickness. Some people amuse themselves when ill with continuous moaning. The forty days of Lent might be annually spent in visiting adjacent tribes and bearing unavoidable hunger and thirst with a good grace. Considering the greatness of the object to be attained, men might go without sugar, coffee, tea, etc. I went from September 1866, to December 1868, without any.

He also gave us a vivid summary of his impressions of the slave system, assuring us that "in sober seriousness, the subject does not admit of exaggeration. To overdraw its evils is a simple impossibility. The sights I have seen, though common incidents of the traffic, are so nauseous that I always try to drive them from memory. In the case of the most disagreeable recollections I can succeed, in time, in consigning them to oblivion, but the slaving scenes come back unbidden, and make me start up at dead of night horrified by their vividness."

August came, and still no arrivals. There was a charming description of the African children and their sports and games, followed by observations on the swallows and the spiders. Then he broke off to exclaim: "That is the atonement of Christ. It is Himself. It is the inherent and everlasting mercy of God made apparent to human eyes and ears. The everlasting love was disclosed by our Lord's life and death. It showed that God forgives because He loves to forgive. He works by smiles, if possible; if not, by frowns.

Pain is only a means of enforcing love."

At last, on August 14, the miserable suspense was at an end. The new expedition marched safely into Unyanyembe. Livingstone lifted up his heart in gratitude to God. Many of those who had come to help him had marched with Stanley and were well-seasoned. Some were Nassick men from Bombay, among whom were John and Jacob Wainwright. It will never be forgotten how much is owed to the intelligence and courage of the latter. Five only in the new expedition belonged to Livingstone's "original followers." These were Susi, Chumah, Amoda, Mabruki, and Gardner. It was much to know that Livingstone was never more loyally and devotedly served than during this last march, which was to have so sad a termination and so heroic a sequel.

> He also gave us a vivid summary of his impressions of the slave system, assuring us that "in sober seriousness, the subject does not admit of exaggeration. To overdraw its evils is a simple impossibility.

Ten days were allowed for rest and preparations for departure, which included the setting aside of certain supplies to await them on the homeward march. Then, on August 25, they slipped quietly out of the town of which Livingstone was so weary and started for the southern part of Lake Tanganyika. We are beginning now the last journey, which ended eight and a half months later, after incredible toils and sufferings. It is difficult to estimate the exact length of it, for there were many short diversions. One need only remember that from the middle of September David Livingstone was to all intents and purposes a dying man. The internal hemorrhage began again, and the entry in his diary on September 19 was that for eight days he had eaten nothing. No rest and no medicines had any lasting effect upon him after this, and he could scarcely have been out of pain, which frequently amounted to agony. At first, they made their way mainly through forest and hilly country, passing from village to village, each day having its burden of travel, its problem of supplies. Livingstone found the climbing "very sore on legs and lungs." On the eighth of October, his eyes rested once again on the blue waters of Tanganyika. The day heat was very trying. Some of the men were sick; all were tired. "Inwardly I feel tired too."

They had come to Tanganyika by a circuitous route. They now kept to the highlands running southwest and traveled along the ridge 1,000 feet above the lake. He noted that the lakeside was favorable for cotton and admired the glory of the sunsets. The various arms and bays of the lake were carefully observed. The route was still very mountainous and painfully up and down. October was past before he reached the part where the lake narrowed and became what the natives call Lake Liemba. It was slow and weary work around the southern section. The heat was intense. "The sun makes the soil so hot that the radiation is as if it came from a furnace. It burns the feet of the people and knocks them up. Subcutaneous[14] inflammation is frequent in the legs, and makes some of my most hardy men useless." He maintained that walking was better than riding. Suddenly he broke off his description of the toilsomeness of the journey to set this down:

> The spirit of Missions is the spirit of our Master, the very genesis of His religion. A diffusive philanthropy is Christianity itself. It requires perpetual propagation to attest its genuineness.

The day after this he was "ill and losing much blood." Another disaster was that the large donkey which had borne him from time to time over difficult ground had been badly bitten by tsetse flies, was now useless, and soon died. "It is a great loss to me."

From the southern extremity of the lake, they proceeded almost due south, the main difficulty being provided by the Lofu River, over which they built a bridge. A little further south they turned westward, evidently making for the north of Lake Bangweulu. Many rivers were crossed, and more hilly regions negotiated. Then came an entry in the journal in so shaky a hand as to be almost indecipherable. It simply tells us that he was ill and camping "in a deserted village." Yet there was no halting on the march. River after river was crossed, and on December 18 he saw once more his old friend the Kalongosi or Kalongwese River. "We crossed it in small

---

[14] That which is situated or introduced under the skin; subdermal.

canoes, and swamped one twice, but no one was lost." They then marched south for the lake. Christmas Day—"our great day"—was cold and wet, but it inspired Livingstone's thanks to "the good Lord for the good gift of His Son, Christ Jesus our Lord." He also found time for some meditations on the Blue and the White Nile. The end of the year brought very heavy weather, during which no observations could be taken. One of the men also was taken critically ill and died. They planted four trees at the corners of the grave.

As the expedition drew near Lake Bangweulu, they came upon a region composed of "spongy morass." The men described it as endless plunging in and out of morasses, and the effect on their strength and spirits must be imagined. It was terrible work, and Livingstone was spent with chronic dysentery. On they went, however, plunging through this horrible country. Yet such alleviations as nature affords was not forgotten. Livingstone enumerated all the flowers he saw: the marigolds and the jonquils, the orchids and the clematis, the gladioli and the flowering bulbs. He rejoiced also to distinguish balsams and "pretty flowery aloes, yellow and red, in one whorl of blossoms." The world is clearly not forsaken that has these tokens of the divine presence.

A week of priceless time was lost in the middle of January owing to the misrepresentations of a chief called Chungu; all the while they were marching aimlessly over the desperate spongy countryside. They had to get back to their starting point and strike eastward to make a circuit of the lake. Livingstone had to be carried across many of the morasses and rivers on the shoulders of one or another of his men. The march was at times almost impossible. January 23 saw them quite lost. No observations could be taken, and it was "rain, rain, rain." Then came January 24 and this dramatic entry in the journal:

> Carrying me across one of the broad, deep, sedgy rivers is really a very difficult task. One we crossed was at least 2,000 feet broad. The first part, the main stream, came up to Susi's mouth, and wetted my seat and legs. One held up my pistol behind, then one after another took a turn, and when he sank into an elephant's deep footprints he required two to lift him.... Every ten or twelve paces brought us to a clear stream, flowing fast in its own channel,

while over all a strong current came bodily through all the rushes
and aquatic plants. Susi had the first spell; then Farijala; then a
tall, stout, Arab-looking man; then Amoda; then Chanda; then
Wadé Salé and each time I was lifted off bodily and put on another pair of stout, willing shoulders, and fifty yards put them out
of breath—no wonder!

We are not surprised to learn that progress was "distressingly
slow; wet, wet, wet, sloppy weather truly, and no observations."
January closed miserably. They had no proper guides. "It is drop,
drop, drop, and drizzling from the northwest." The country was all
froths and sponges. Livingstone lost much blood but, with characteristic optimism, expressed the hope that it was a safety valve, for
he had no fever.

The lack of guides was serious. Livingstone reckoned they lost
half a month floundering about in this sodden, depressing country,
suffering much hunger, and it was all due to the unfriendliness of
some and the fear of others. When guides were ultimately obtained,
progress was far more speedy and direct; but what the fatigue and
exposure meant to the sick man can be best gauged by the note in
the journal on February 14, which followed the record of another
"excessive hemorrhagic discharge."

> If the good Lord gives me favor, and permits me to finish my work
> I shall thank and bless Him, though it costs me untold toil, pain
> and travel; this trip has made my hair all grey.

Melancholy as the last month has been, it is perhaps not so
heartbreaking as the next. It represents the almost desperate exertions of a dying man to get on; yet he was thwarted and deceived at
every turn. He fixed his hopes on Chief Matipa, and on the twenty-
second of February sent Susi and Chumah to find him. Matipa
appeared to be friendly, and eventually the expedition traveled by
canoes towards his country. Then they had to cross flooded prairie
and camp on a "miserable, dirty, fishy island." They arrived at last,
and Matipa was profuse in his promises and plausible in his plans.
Time was of no value to Matipa. He drowned his cares in "pombe";
but Livingstone was in misery. Day after day passed, and no promised canoes arrived to carry the expedition westward. By the eigh-

teenth of March he was convinced that Matipa was "acting the villain." The next day was his birthday and sacred to other thoughts. "Thanks to the Almighty Preserver of man for sparing me thus far on the journey of life. Can I hope for ultimate success? So many obstacles have arisen. Let not Satan prevail over me, O my good Lord Jesus!"

Never had he been in a worse case. Matipa was false again, and Livingstone took the extreme step, for him, of making a demonstration in force and firing a pistol through the roof of the chief's house—a movement which resulted in Matipa's flight. He returned, however, soon after in a chastened frame of mind. Some canoes being available at last on March 24, Livingstone started with all his goods, his object being to get across the Chambezé. It was an awful journey. Six hours of punting brought them to a little islet without a tree, and the rain descended pitilessly. They got what shelter they could out of an inverted canoe and crouched under it. The wind tore the tent and damaged it. The loads were soaked. It was bitterly cold. "A man put my bed into the bilge and never said 'Bail out,' so I am safe for a wet night, but it turned out better than I expected."

March 28th. — Nothing earthly will make me give up my work in despair. I encourage myself in the Lord my God and go forward.

The next day brought them across the Chambezé, but progress was extremely slow and it was the fifth of April before the neighboring river, Lobingela, was passed. Meanwhile, as we learn from a subsequent entry in the diary, his final critical illness had begun. On March 31 an artery began "bleeding profusely." Yet he did not dream of resting. The whole country round Lake Bangweulu was a shallow sea. It was impossible to say where the rivers began and ended. Livingstone's mode of progression was being punted along in a canoe. Further inland there was a marching party struggling along parallel with the canoes. On April 10, he set down that he was pale and bloodless. The artery "gives off a copious stream and takes away my strength. Oh! how I long to be permitted by the Over Power to finish my work." The seventeenth of April witnessed another calamity, when "a tremendous rain after dark burst all our now rotten tents in shreds."

He was now utterly weak and ill, fighting his complaint with quinine and trying to believe it was no more than fever. On the nineteenth, however, he confessed he was "excessively weak, and but for the donkey could not move a hundred yards." He added humorously, "it is not all pleasure this exploration."

The diary was now painful reading—the writing becomes very shaky, eloquent of weakness and pain. He had service on Sunday, April 20 as usual. The last entries are quite short.

> **April 21st.** — Tried to ride but was forced to lie down, and they carried me back to vil., exhausted.

The fact is that the old hero insisted on being put on his donkey, only to fall to the ground. He was carried back to the halting-place on Chumah's shoulders.

> **April 22nd.** — Carried on kitanda, over Buga, S.W. 2 1/4.

The men made a rude palanquin,[15] covered it with grass and a blanket, and in this way carried the dying chief for two hours and a quarter. They were two and a quarter hours of excruciating agony, and it was a relief to all when a village was reached where a rude hut could be erected.

The next day was similar. They carried him for another hour and a half. The following day, one hour's journey was all that he, in his extreme emaciation, could endure. He was too weak now to write anything except the date. On the twenty-fifth, they proceeded for an hour and found themselves among a simple, friendly people. The trend of Livingstone's thoughts may be gathered by some questions he addressed to the natives. He wanted to know whether they had ever heard of a hill on which four rivers had their rise. They shook their heads but confessed themselves no travelers. On the following day they still moved on, and Livingstone's unconquerable hope appeared in the fact that he instructed Susi to buy two large tusks because he might be short of goods when they got back to Ujiji, and he could buy cloth of the Arabs with them.

The last entry in the diary, the last words he ever wrote, stand under the date April 27, 1873:

---

[15] A covered litter, usually for one person, carried by poles on the shoulders of two or more men.

April 27th. — Knocked up quite and remain—recover—sent to buy milch [i.e., milk-giving] goats. — We are on the banks of the Molilamo.

He was lying at Kolunganjovu's town. His one hope was in milk, but the search for milch goats was vain. The whole district had been plundered by the Mazitu. He tried to eat a little pounded corn but failed. The twenty-eighth was spent in similar vain endeavors to obtain milk. On the twenty-ninth, the chief, who said "everything should be done for his friend," offered to escort the caravan to the crossing-place and see them provided with canoes. There was an initial difficulty. Livingstone could not walk to the door of the hut to reach his litter. The wall was opened and the sick man transferred from his bed to the litter in that way. The narrative of his devoted men is now most explicit. It is eloquent alike of the great leader's fortitude and their own unfailing consideration. We need not linger on the details; the agony of lifting him into the canoe and lifting him out; the journey through "swamps and plashes [i.e., shallow pools]"; the arrival at Chitambo's village; the delays in building the hut while he lay "under the broad eaves of a native hut" and a soft drizzle of rain descended. At last the shelter was erected and banked round with earth; the bed was made, raised on sticks and grass, the medicine chest placed on a large box that did duty for a table, and a fire kindled outside opposite the door. Just inside, the boy Majwara lay down and slept, that he might be at hand if wanted.

The imagination reverently dwells on every detail of the scene, for the old hero has made his last journey and is about to sleep his last sleep. While he was lying on his litter outside and the rain was falling, curious villagers had gathered round, each man with bow in hand, for they had been guarding their crops. This was the great chief who had come from far. His fame they knew somewhat; they could not know that he was the best friend Africa ever had. They gazed respectfully and wonderingly at the thin, pale, emaciated sufferer with the bloodless hands and lips, and the face distorted with sharp throes of agony. Through the falling rain they watched him and in days to come would tell

He was lying, stretched forward across the bed, in the attitude of prayer, his head buried in his hands. None seemed to dare to approach him for a while. Then Matthew, reverently and tremblingly, stretched out his hand and laid it on his master's cheek. It was quite cold. David Livingstone was dead. It was the morning of the fourth of May 1873.

their children that they had seen Livingstone.

That night passed quietly and when Chitambo called next day, Livingstone, with unfailing courtesy, received him, though he had to beg the chief to go away and return on the following day when he hoped to feel stronger. All that morning he lay suffering, his strength gradually ebbing. In the afternoon he bade Susi bring him his watch, and with great effort he slowly wound it. Night fell at last, and at eleven o'clock Livingstone called Susi. There were noises heard. "Are our men making those noises?" said Livingstone. Susi told him that the villagers were scaring a buffalo. "Is this the Luapula?" he asked again, and Susi knew that his master was wandering in his mind. How ardently he had desired to reach the Luapula through those terrible weeks and months on the sponges and through the floods! When Susi told him where they were, he asked again, "How many days to the Luapula?" "I think it is three days," said Susi. There was no more except the cry of pain, "Oh, dear, dear!" Then he dozed. Near midnight he sent for Susi again. This time Livingstone told him to boil some water; when Susi had filled the copper kettle he again asked for the medicine chest. The candle had to be held close to him, for his eyes were very dim, but he did just succeed in selecting some calomel[16] which he wanted to have at his side with a little water in a cup.

Then he said, very faintly, "All right! you can go now." These were the last words he was heard to speak. It almost seemed as if a higher Master had said to His tired servant, "All right! You can go now."

---

[16] Mercurous chloride, HgCl—a white, tasteless powder, formerly used as a purging for intestinal worms.

What happened after that is known only to the One who was with him at the last. The boy Majwara slept, and while he slept the miracle happened. For it appeared miraculous and incredible to his men, who had seen his utter inability to move himself, that he did actually rise from off that rude couch and did kneel down at the side, his knees probably on the bare soil, and there in the attitude of prayer commended himself to God, "And his fair soul unto his Captain Christ."

When the lad Majwara awoke at 4:00 a.m. and saw the strange sight of his master kneeling thus, he was afraid, and slipped out to warn the others. Susi dared not go in alone. He ran to rouse Chumah, Chowperé, Matthew, and Nuanyaséré. The six stood awestruck at the door of the little hut. On the box a candle was burning. It was just stuck there in its own wax, but it relieved the darkness; and they gazed at the still, bowed form. He was lying, stretched forward across the bed, in the attitude of prayer, his head buried in his hands. None seemed to dare to approach him for a while. Then Matthew, reverently and tremblingly, stretched out his hand and laid it on his master's cheek. It was quite cold. David Livingstone was dead. It was the morning of the fourth of May 1873.

With the death of the hero, most biographies quickly end. In this respect Livingstone's story is wholly unique. The most thrilling and sensational chapter remains to be written. Nothing more convincingly illustrates Livingstone's ascendancy over his followers than the events which followed his death. It would have been easy for the men to have hurried the body into the ground, divided the property among themselves, and dispersed to their homes. Perhaps the last thing to be expected was that they would shoulder the dead body and carry it from the center of Africa more than a thousand miles, through hostile and inhospitable country, to the ocean. Yet this was what they did; while the method, order, and reverence of their proceedings would have done honor to the wisest and most civilized of our race. Let us now see how they faced the duty that had suddenly come to them.

The discovery of Livingstone's death was made about 4:00 a.m. The news was carried round at once to all the men, and as soon as

day dawned they assembled for conference. The dead man's possessions were collected, the boxes opened in the presence of all, and
Jacob Wainwright made a careful and exact inventory on a page of
Livingstone's little metallic pocket book, in which his own last entries had been made. The next business was to appoint Susi and
Chumah, the oldest and most experienced of Livingstone's followers, as leaders of the expedition. All promised to obey their orders,
and all kept their word. Fearing lest the native superstitions in regard to departed spirits might lead to some outrage on the dead
body, or that Chitambo might demand some ruinous fine, they
decided to conceal for the present the fact of the death. In this respect they had misjudged Chitambo, who soon learned what had
happened and proved himself the kindest and most sympathetic of
advisers. All were agreed that the body of Livingstone must be carried back to the coast.

The first practical step after making the inventory was a remarkable one. Outside Chitambo's village the men erected a small
settlement of their own, fortified by a stockade. Here they built a
circular hut, open to the sky, but strong enough to resist any attack
of wild beasts, and in this they laid the body of Livingstone. His
followers were stationed all round like a guard of honor. It happened that Farijala had once been servant to a Zanzibar doctor and
knew the elementary facts about a postmortem. With the assistance
of a Nassick man named Carras, he undertook to do what was necessary. Certain rites of mourning having been performed, and vol-
leys fired, a screen was held over these men while they did their
work. The heart and viscera (internal organs) were removed, placed
in a tin box, and reverently buried four feet in the ground, while
Jacob Wainwright read the Burial Service from the English Prayer
Book. The body was then dried in the sun for fourteen days. So
emaciated was it that there was little more than skin and bone. For
a coffin, they stripped the bark off a Myonga tree in one piece; the
corpse was carefully enveloped in calico (plain white cotton cloth)
and inserted in the bark cylinder. The whole was sewn up in a piece
of sailcloth (light cotton canvas) and lashed to a pole, so that it
could be carried on the men's shoulders. Then Jacob Wainwright

carved Livingstone's name and the date of his death on the tree standing near where the body rested. Chitambo was charged to keep the ground free from grass lest bush-fires should burn the tree. Finally they erected two strong posts, with a cross beam, and covered them thoroughly with tar so that the spot might be definitely identified. They seem to have forgotten nothing that could be done to keep in perpetual memory the place where Livingstone breathed his last.

> Nothing more convincingly illustrates Livingstone's ascendancy over his followers than the events which followed his death. … Perhaps the last thing to be expected was that they would shoulder the dead body and carry it from the center of Africa more than a thousand miles, through hostile and inhospitable country, to the ocean. Yet this was what they did.

The line of march chosen was up the west coast of Lake Bangweulu and across the Luapula River, then northeastward until they struck the route by which they had come from Unyanyembe. It seemed at the outset as if all their hopes were to be frustrated. In three days, half the expedition were down with fever. Two women died. Susi became critically ill and could not move. They were delayed a whole month and only started again to break down once more. It was not till they had crossed the great Luapula River—four miles broad—that things went better with them. Near where the Liposhosi River flows into the lake at Chawende's village, the expedition was unfortunately brought into active conflict with the chief and his tribe, and a regular battle took place in which blood was shed and many native houses burned. It is probable that a calmer and stronger leadership might have averted this, but it was proof of the determination of the devoted band to defend their precious burden with their lives.

After this, the march was, on the whole, a favorable and peaceful one. They turned north towards Tanganyika, but, profiting by previous experience, gave the lake itself a wide berth, keeping well to the east, and traveling far more easily than Livingstone had done owing to the fact that they largely avoided the mountainous region. Everywhere the news of Livingstone's death had preceded them, and they were made aware that a party of Englishmen was at Unyanyembe awaiting their arrival. Jacob Wainwright wrote down the story as we know it, and Chumah hurried on by forced marches to deliver it to the Englishmen in question, who turned out to be Lieutenant Cameron, Dr. Dillon, and Lieutenant Murphy, members of a search "expedition." To them, on October 20, 1873, Chumah brought the news, and soon afterwards the gallant band arrived and delivered all Livingstone's belongings intact to his fellow countrymen.

Lieutenant Cameron was decidedly in favor of burying the body in African soil; he also took the liberty of appropriating most of Livingstone's instruments to the use of his expedition. This latter act the men were powerless to resist, but in regard to the former they were not to be moved. It was useless to argue with them as to the disturbed district between Unyanyembe and the coast. They had made up their minds that the great Doctor must "go home." Lieutenant Murphy and Dr. Dillon decided to return to Zanzibar with them, and the former does not appear to have been a very amicable companion. Dr. Dillon's tragic end is well known. Seized with fever on the journey, he went out of his mind and committed suicide.

One further incident has to be recorded which is illustrative of the resolution and ingenuity of the members of the expedition. Near Kasekera matters developed threateningly, and the men became convinced that there would be growing hostility along the route to the passage of a dead body. They accordingly resorted to a ruse. They unpacked the body, and repacked it to look like an ordinary bale of goods. Then they filled the old cylinder with sticks and grasses and solemnly dispatched six men back to Unyanyembe to bury it! Needless to say, as soon as these men got well into the jungle they disposed of their burden and rejoined the main caravan by devious routes. So well did every man keep his counsel, that it was believed henceforth that ordinary merchandise was being carried to Zanzibar.

On February 15, 1874, their sacred charge was fulfilled, and their precious burden, so jealously and triumphantly preserved, was handed over to the possession of the British Consul at Bagamoio on the coast. The *Calcutta* transferred the remains to Aden, and the steamer *Malwa* carried them thence to Southampton, where on April 15 a special train was in waiting to convey them to London. That evening they were deposited in the rooms of the Geographical Society in Savile Row and examined by Sir William Fergusson and other medical gentlemen. The "oblique fracture" of the arm which had been broken by the lion so many years before, and the false joint that had resulted, provided ample identification of the remains. On Saturday, April 18, they were borne through the crowded streets of the capital to Westminster Abbey and deposited in the center of the nave. Among the pallbearers were several who had been closely identified with the great explorer—Mr. Stanley, Dr. Kirk, Mr. Webb, Mr. Oswell, Mr. Young, and not least Jacob Wainwright, the Nassick man. In the vast congregation there was no nobler or more striking figure than Livingstone's father-in-law, the veteran Dr. Moffat, the father of her who "sleeps on Shupanga brae...." No grave in the famous Abbey is more frequently asked for by visitors than his. It makes its solemn appeal to the world year after year, for the plain slab is extraordinarily happy in its inscription:

Brought by faithful hands
Over land and sea,
Here Rests
DAVID LIVINGSTONE,
Missionary, Traveller, Philanthropist.
Born March 19, 1813,
At Blantyre, Lanarkshire.
Died May 4th, 1873,
At Chitambo's Village, Ilala.

For thirty years his life was spent
in an unwearied effort to evangelise
the native races, to explore the
undiscovered secrets,
And abolish the desolating slave
trade of Central Africa, where, with
his last words, he wrote:
"All I can say in my solitude is,
may Heaven's rich blessing come
down on every one—American,
English, Turk—who will help to
heal the open sore of the world.

Along the right border of the stone ran the happily chosen words:

*Tantus amor veri, nihil est quod
noscere malim
Quam fluvii causas,
per saecula tanta latentes.*

And along the left border:

"Other sheep I have which are
not of this fold, them also I must
bring, and they shall hear my voice."

— Epilogue —

The life of Livingstone has been carefully told in general terms, although the personality of the man has not often appeared in these pages. It is believed, therefore, that the reader will welcome a few personal details that could not well find a place in previous chapters. The portrait of Livingstone is well-known. It is a strong, rugged face, rather heavy and severe in its general effect, with a thick dark mustache, a broad mouth and full chin—the whole lightened, however, by honest kindly eyes and the suggestion of humor about the lips. When he was a young man it would appear that his hair was almost black, but it became lighter in color later, and the lock of it in possession of one of his relatives is distinctly brown. He is himself our authority for saying that his beard was reddish in color, and it must be remembered that in this respect all our pictures are at fault. Not one of them shows us a bearded African traveler, yet, except on his visits to England, he always wore a beard. Stanley's first impression was of the grey-bearded man whom he found at Ujiji. Later on he noted that his hair had still a "brownish color," but that his beard and mustache were "very grey." Stanley also paid a tribute to the brightness of his eyes, which he says were hazel. They appear to have been grey with a bluish tinge. Livingstone himself comments on the astonishment of the natives at his red beard and blue eyes. From that reference one might imagine that he had the appearance of a Viking or Scandinavian; but the fact is that his eyes were really more grey than blue, and that his hair was a very dark brown, while his beard was more distinctively "sandy."

In height he always appeared quite short when in contact with tall companions. Nevertheless, he was about average height, say five feet six inches; certainly not more. He had the broad chest and shoulders of a man specially built to endure exceptional fatigue, but otherwise he always created the impression of a short and lean man. That he inherited an iron constitution is evident from the mere narrative of his travels and privations. One of the things that most vividly impressed Stanley was how swiftly the man he found—so worn and thin and haggard—threw off the burden of the years, recovered his old buoyancy of spirit and physical efficiency, and took upon him the appearance of one who was ten years younger than his actual age.

He was in some ways a fastidious person. He was scrupulously neat in his manner of dress. Even on his travels, when making his way through swamp and jungle, the one luxury he most prized was a change of raiment; and his torn clothes would be mended to the best of his ability. Stanley found him "dressed in a red shirt, with a crimson cap trimmed by a gold band, an old tweed pair of pants, and shoes looking the worse for wear."

Dr. Livingstone's operating bag

The wonder is he had anything left that was fit to be seen, and the new apparel that came to him was hailed with genuine exclamations of delight. He placed great worth on being an example of simplicity and neatness to the natives. This characteristic also comes out in other ways. His diaries are done with wonderful care and precision. His handwriting was not naturally good, but it is admirably legible.

Every entry in his diary bears upon it the marks of method and neatness, while the scientific observations are set forth with a clearness which won the highest praise from those best competent to give it. Nothing was slurred over. There is no sign of hurry or of the exhaustion of patience. Similarly, there is a notable absence of all embroidery. The language is throughout austerely plain and truthful. Everything is in keeping with his essential character—a man who hated the vulgarity of useless or tawdry rhetoric and held always by the refinement of simplicity. From many anecdotes related of him, it is clear that not only his writing but his private and public speech were affected by his taste in this respect. A letter is well-known in which he counseled his children to speak English because it was "prettier" than the Scottish language. He was doubtless thinking of the somewhat coarse Scottish accent prevalent in Glasgow and the neighborhood where his youth was spent. Strangers who met him were uniformly impressed by the softness and gentleness of his speech. His voice was deep, and if sometimes in public it took on a harsh sound, this was undoubtedly due to the difficulty of public utterance, which he never mastered. His addresses to great audiences in England were always delivered in a slow, hesitating, and rather labored fashion. For one thing, he grew so accustomed to thinking and speaking in the native languages of Africa that his own tongue became strange to him. Apart from that, he was never a fluent speaker; public address was an ordeal to him. He had a Puritan disposition towards restraint and reserve, combined with a scientific predilection for exact statement. The impression he left upon his audience, however, was always powerful. Everyone who

heard him testifies that the man triumphed where the orator often failed.

When he once became sufficiently at home with anyone to conquer his natural reserve, he was excellent company for he had a large fund of humor and the gift

Livingstone's instrument case

of Teufelsdröckian laughter—"a laugh of the whole man from heel to head." He was especially devoted to children. One correspondent remembers him most vividly with a child on each knee telling them lion stories. Another recalls his own boyhood and days of sickness in bed, brightened by a visit from Livingstone who showed him the marks of the lion's teeth in his arm and entertained him with some of his adventures. The atmosphere that he most detested was the atmosphere of flattery. There is a fine story about him which illustrates this. He had been invited out to dinner and had fallen to the lot of a society lady who was injudicious enough to indulge in some very highly colored compliments on his achievements. Suddenly Livingstone left the table and was afterwards discovered sitting in a room in the dark. He explained that he could not endure to be praised to his face, and that he would not sit and listen to it. One who knew him intimately told me of a lecture delivered in one of our great northern towns. Two local orators introduced the proceedings with speeches magnifying Livingstone's achievements. When he rose to his feet he had an overwhelming reception, but, turning straight to a large map, he said in a singularly cold, hard voice: "If you want to know the truth about the river system of Central Africa, be good enough to look at this map," and plunged into his subject without a word of reference to anything that had been said about himself. He was the least vain and most unspoiled of any man who was ever lionized by the British public, the secret of which was undoubtedly to be found in the humility and sincerity of his Christian faith and character.

Of that faith something ought to be said. In his earliest letters which have been preserved, we can see how strongly he was influenced by forms of biblical theology that have long since ceased to be regarded as applicable by many liberal theologians and modern missionaries. That the heathen who had never heard of Christ were perishing eternally was a doctrine that inspired much missionary devotion in Livingstone's day as well as the belief in the ultimate triumph of the Kingdom of God prior to Christ's second coming. These truths, it is clear, very gradually became Livingstone's only abiding pillars of inspiration as he faced the actual challenges of the vast heathen world. In a letter written just at the time of his ordination, he expresses his sense of the honor done to him in being accepted by Christ Jesus as one of His witnesses. The absolute surrender of his own will and mind to "his fair Captain Christ" was the fact most fundamental to Livingstone's whole career. To the last, he never felt that he was really in the way of duty unless he was doing missionary work and bearing witness to the lordship of Christ. Stanley bore his testimony to the practical character of Livingstone's religion. "In him religion exhibits its loveliest features; it governs his conduct not only towards his servants, but towards the natives, the [Muslims], and all who come in contact with him." In another striking phrase, he says: "Religion has tamed him and made him a Christian gentleman." Until his physical powers utterly failed, he never omitted to gather his men around him for evening service, read and pray with them, and add some simple exhortation.

He was a man of deep convictions. Once thoroughly alive to some fact, he took a tenacious grip of it and gave it a place in all his thinking. That was how it came to pass that neither the politicians nor the men of science could prevail upon him to leave the social sore of Africa to others and devote himself to exploration and discovery. Livingstone's Puritan soul, that knew how to put first things in the first place, realized that the fact of most importance in Africa was not the sources of the Nile, but the sources of the slave trade. This great social problem had to be attacked if religious and spiritual work was not to be undermined. Much might be written about his courage in alienating those who sympathized with his work as an explorer and those who might have assisted him financially. He knew quite well that a price must be paid by anyone who was really in earnest to destroy the slave trade, but nothing moved him. Henceforth it was a case of "this one thing I do." Perhaps the most remarkable fact of all is, how early in his life he perceived that here lay the path he was to tread. There is an old, brown, and much-torn letter which must have been the first he wrote from the Cape on his arrival there, and is dated March 10, 1841. Every inch of the large sheet is covered with writing, and among the last words is a reference to the resistance of certain of the Boers to the policy of emancipation. Then follows this sentence: "Oh! when shall the time come in which every man that feels the heat of the sun shall be freed from all other fetters but bonds of love to our Savior!" So the young missionary wrote in his first letter from Africa; so he prayed and strove for thirty laborious and weary years, and so he prays still from his new home in heaven, and few will claim that that prayer has been vainly uttered in the ear of God and man.

His unique influence over the natives of Africa is admitted. It may not be possible wholly to analyze his secret, for such words as "personality" and "magnetism" are easily written and do not help us very much. Two things we may say on this subject, and leave it. Firstly, he believed in them; and secondly, he did not expect too much of them. This is no more than to say that he entered into his inheritance by means of the two ancient and Scriptural keys—faith and patience. He was abundantly rewarded for his faith. "Any one," he said once, "who lives long among them (i.e., the natives) forgets that they are black and remembers only that they are fellowmen." That was certainly all that he remembered. The stories of Sechéle, Sebituane, Sekelétu, and others would have set the crown on his reputation were it not that that was reserved for the heroic band who attended him on the last of his journeys and made themselves an everlasting name by their final and supreme act of devotion. Nevertheless, if he saw their splendid possibilities underneath all their degradation, he never expected too much of them. His scientific mind appreciated all that they owed to centuries of savagery and superstition. He was infinitely patient with them. He forgave them until seventy times seven. He quietly and gently reasoned with them when any other white man would have lost his temper and resorted to force. He could hardly be persuaded even to punish the prodigal sons in his midst with any severity. "I have faults myself," he would say simply.

The last word should concern his single-mindedness and disinterestedness. Neither as missionary nor as Government official is there any trail of commercialism over his life. When the bank in Bombay failed, with the money he had lodged in its keeping, it hardly cost him a pang. All his money was dedicated to the cause in which he gave his life, and his personal serenity was quite independent of possessions. He refused to bargain with the Government as to terms, and when Lord Palmerston sent a friend to ask what he could do for him, Livingstone's whole ambitions were centered on an international arrangement that would sanction the creation of settlements which could stand between the natives and the slavers. At no single period in his life is there any bit of evidence that he cared for money save as it might advance the cause that was dearer to him than life itself.

The world still argues and disputes as to what it is that constitutes the highest form of greatness. In the common accepted meaning of the term, Livingstone was not a man of genius. He was not brilliant; he was not strikingly original. What he achieved was done by the simple Christian virtue of compassion—he cared for people, body and soul. Nevertheless, this we may surely say: If human greatness consists not in any natural endowment alone, but rather in all the powers and faculties of a man's nature brought into subjection to one supreme and unselfish ambition for the glory of God and the good of man, then few greater men have ever walked this earth than David Livingstone.

In regard to the field of Christian missions faithful men like Moffat, Cary, and Livingstone were used by God to help define the true scope that missionary work should encompass. The modern missionary movements of the twentieth century, within conservative Protestant circles, adopted the model for missionary involvement that was lived out by men like Livingstone. As usual, David Livingstone's own words give us a clear understanding of his approach to missionary work and to the Christian life:

> Nowhere have I ever appeared as anything else but a servant of God, who has simply followed the leadings of His hand. My views of what is missionary duty are not so contracted as those whose ideal is a dumpy sort of man with a Bible under his arm. I have laboured in bricks and mortar; at the forge and carpenter's bench, as well as in preaching and medical practice. I feel that I am "not on my own." I am serving Christ when shooting a buffalo for my men, or taking an astronomical observation.

May the same Lord who raised up David Livingstone be pleased to grant the Church a new legion of faithful men for Kingdom work in the twenty-first century!

"I beg to direct your attention to Africa;
I know that in a few years
I shall be cut off in that country,
which is now open:
do not let it be shut again!

I go back to Africa
to try to make an open path
for commerce and Christianity;
it is for you to carry out the work
which I have begun. I leave it with you!"

—David Livingstone

— Index —

V

Victoria Falls 50, 61

W

Wainwright, Jacob 103, 112, 114,
    115
Wainwright, John 103
Wardlaw, Rev. Dr. 7
Water snakes 29
Wayau men 71
Webb, Mr. 68, 87, 115
Westminster Abbey 8, 100, 115
Wilberforce, William 4

Y

Yao tribe xii
Young, E. D. 75, 87, 115
Young, James 69

Z

Zalanyama range 75
Zambezi River xi, 27, 30, 33,
    45, 46, 47, 51, 56, 58, 59,
    62, 69, 72
Zanzibar 47, 65, 72, 86, 92, 99
Zimbabwe 48
Zouga River 21–22, 23